£1.24

The Cross in the Experience of our Lord

R. A. Finlayson

Christian Focus Publications

© Christian Focus Publications Ltd
ISBN 1 85792 029 X

Originally published in 1955
This edition published in 1993
by
Christian Focus Publications Ltd
Geanies House, Fearn, Ross-shire,
IV20 1TW, Scotland, Great Britain.

Printed and bound in Great Britain by
Cox & Wyman Ltd, Reading, Berkshire

Cover design
by
Donna Macleod

CONTENTS

Biographical introduction

Tradition has it that one celebrated divine when responding to a publisher's request for sermon material, counselled his literary patron, 'Mr Printer, do your work quickly, for preachers are soon forgotten!' Sadly, experience confirms the accuracy of this pessimistic generalisation. For author and for publisher alike, the rewards from printed sermons rank far down the scale of literary remuneration. Yet, preachers ought not to be so readily consigned to oblivion for the Epistle to the Hebrews urges its readers to keep in mind the memory of their departed guides, those who had spoken to them the Word of God and who had made known to them the way of life from the Word of Life (Hebrews 13:7). That exhortation is itself sufficient justification for reprinting this choice specimen of the preaching gifts of one who, in his day, was a source of blessing to many.

Roderick Alick Finlayson was born on 18 November 1895 to Roderick Finlayson, merchant at Lochcarron, and his wife Christy MacLennan, the family home being situated at Hazelbrae on the western extremity of the picturesque village of Lochcarron which straddles the northern shore of the sea loch in Wester Ross from which the village is named. When the mother gave birth, the father was ill with pneumonia and it is said that Roderick, his only son, was baptised over his father's coffin.

Down the years Lochcarron has been the scene of many notable ministries, among them that of Aeneas Sage (1694-

1774) whose physical prowess no less than his spiritual vigour was deployed to subdue the passions of his unruly parishioners. Another spiritual genius, whose exploits on behalf of the Kingdom of God are still spoken of in the locality, was Lachlan Mackenzie (1754-1819) or 'Mister Lachlan' as he was invariably called. Neither of these men was a native of Lochcarron but the community itself gave rise to several notable churchmen such as Donald Kennedy of Kishorn, an elder and close associate of Mister Lachlan, and the progenitor of an eminent line of Highland ministers which included Dr John Kennedy of Dingwall (1819-1884). Kishorn was also the birthplace of the Rev Murdo Mackenzie (1835-1912), minister of the Free North Church, Inverness, who, more than any other churchman, influenced the Free Church in the Highlands to remain loyal to her Disruption testimony during the church union crisis in 1900. Professor Donald Maclean DD (1869-1943), another eminent Free Churchman, was also a native of Lochcarron and so with such a cluster of Free Church luminaries emanating from that small Highland community we can be sure that from an early age R A Finlayson followed the ebb and flow of the church's fortunes with an eager interest.

Like others of his generation Roderick, when he had reached his teens, had to go to Dingwall on the eastern seaboard of Ross to complete his secondary education. There he lived in lodgings on Mill Street and on Sundays he worshipped in the church made famous by Dr John Kennedy. Under the pastoral care of the warmly evangelical Rev Norman Campbell - one of the small band of ministers who remained loyal to the Free Church following the union

5

of 1900 * - Roderick's awareness of the spiritual dimension to life was deepened and intensified.

In October 1912 he matriculated at the University of Aberdeen but with what intention as regards a vocation in life it is not possible to say. Undoubtedly he had developed spiritually under Norman Campbell in Dingwall but it was not until 1915 that he made public profession of his faith by seeking admission to the communicant membership of the Free Church. In later years he himself was given to say to others on the threshold of manhood that he had found it to be a stabilising experience to have made profession of his faith at the Lord's Table. No doubt the timing of his decision was significant for it followed on to the outbreak of the First World War. To a world already adrift on a sea of change there had now been added the perils of war which Roddy and so many of his contemporaries were to face in Flanders fields. It is not surprising then that he felt the urge to identify himself with the people of God as one having laid hold on a 'refuge most secure'. And so in February 1915 he returned from Aberdeen to Dingwall for the communion season and was there received into the membership of the congregation that had known him as a youth and that had watched over, with prayerful interest, his spiritual and intellectual development. He returned to Aberdeen, but by the end of the year he had enlisted with his County Regiment, the Seaforth Highlanders, and some months later he found himself in France with the British Expedi-

---

* In 1900, the majority of Free Church ministers, along with their congregations, united with the United Presbyterian Church to form the United Free Church. Those Free Church ministers and congregations who declined to go in with the majority did so for doctrinal and ecclesiastical reasons.

tionary Force. After being in action for many months he, unlike many of his companions, was spared to return to Aberdeen, although not without the scars of battle, and, resuming his studies, he graduated MA in 1919.

When R A Finlayson first matriculated at Aberdeen, the Professor of English Language and Literature was H J C Grierson, later Sir Herbert Grierson. Teacher and student alike revelled in the beauty of the English language and even at that early stage, Finlayson's giftedness as a literary critic was such that he was urged on completion of his Arts degree to do post-graduate work at Cambridge University. No doubt had he chosen to do so he could have followed a path to honour and greatness of a different kind, but by then he had pledged his allegiance to another teacher and to a higher cause. His delight in literature was now subordinated to serve the interests of the Book of Books, and in October 1919 he enrolled as a student of divinity at the Free Church College, Edinburgh. By 1922 he had completed his training, and as a probationer of the church was eligible to receive a call. Interestingly the first approach that came to him was from his native parish of Lochcarron which, as it happened, became vacant at that time. However, Finlayson, according to the Presbytery's minute, 'though he highly appreciated the people's confidence in him, did not regard it as his duty to be settled in his native parish'. There the matter ended and shortly afterwards he accepted a call to Urray (Muir-of-Ord) in Ross-shire.

In Urray he pursued his ministry in every way possible. With his domestic necessities being attended to by an older sister to whom he was deeply attached, he devoted himself to pastoring his people and to perfecting his preaching ministry. In one important respect he was less than well-equipped for pulpit ministry. In a day prior to the introduction of electronic sound amplification, he had to cope with the handicap of a voice which, although pleasant and distinctive in its West Highland cadence, was lacking in richness and resonance. Even so, the clarity of his enunciation ensured that the listener could follow him without strain.

Out of the pulpit his gift for story-telling made him a most entertaining companion. Although devoid of any capacity for mimicry, his gift for seizing on some individual idiosyncrasy or mannerism enabled him to portray another's character with remarkable and amusing vividness; and that, together with his scintillating wit and his genius for saying a thing well, ensured that company gravitated towards him. He had the ability, had he used it, to have written a series of character sketches of ministers and men of the Highlands that, for impish and incisive description, would have out-rivalled the considerable achievements in that direction of Norman C Macfarlane in his *Apostles of the North* and even challenged for first place the work of the acknowledged genius in the field, Donald Sage in his *Memorabilia Domestica*. Finlayson often contemplated doing such a thing but discretion appears to have prevailed in this instance.

It was of course as a preacher and not as a story-teller that R A Finlayson was revered. He was a powerful preacher, not in terms of voice production, but on account of his ability to make the Scriptures speak powerfully to his hearers. The power which characterised his preaching may be attributed to his personal knowledge of God, his intimate knowledge of Scripture, his intuitive understanding of people and his consummate skill with words. A devout man, ever conscious of his own need of a Saviour and of the power of Christ to save and to satisfy, he was also an exceptionally shrewd judge of character, one who knew instinctively how to get his message home to other minds. Thus equipped he brought out of the treasury of God things new and old in such a way as to captivate any who had the slightest sympathy with his mission and his message. Truths that were old and commonplace he re-stated in such thrilling and felicitous diction as made them take on new lustre, and at the same time, his incisive mind wrested from familiar passages new insights that gave added sparkle to the truth. Yet for all his adroitness of analysis and expression, his appeal was ultimately to the heart rather than to the mind of his hearers. He understood people and their problems, and he brought the healing power of the gospel to bear upon them in a most winsome and affecting way. Favoured indeed was the community of Urray to have enjoyed such a ministry for eighteen years.

For many, the year 1939 saw the passing of the old order and Finlayson, like many others, was called to new spheres of service. The tenor of his way was no longer to be cast in the sequestered vale of rural life. He accepted a call to Hope Street Gaelic Church (now St Vincent Street) in Glasgow. The death of his sister shortly before he left Urray had been a source of great sorrow to him, but in October 1940 his marriage to Miss Rachel Mackay, who came from a Tain family of which several members were already rendering sterling service on behalf of the Free Church both at home and abroad, brought a new and welcome companionship to his life and, in due time, a son in whom he took great delight. His tenure in Hope Street was relatively short and fragmented by secondment from 1941-1944 to the Army Chaplaincy Service in which he rose to be Deputy-Assistant Chaplain-General at Scottish Command.

The welfare of the British soldiery was always at the heart of his affections and his anxious concern for them featured prominently in his public intercession. I recall him at the Assembly of 1971 remarking with great feeling on the fact that at the Wednesday morning hour given to public prayer for the church and nation, not one of those called on to pray had had any thought for the servicemen then under terrorist attack in Ulster. To his mind this was a grave dereliction of duty on the part of the church. He himself was attracted to the comradeship of Army life. The picture of a disciplined body of men enlisting in the service of the King of Kings to endure whatever hardships that service demanded, had great appeal for him. On one occasion during the war he was invited in his capacity as DACG to preach in King's College Chapel, Aberdeen to the Officers Training Corps. Taking as his theme the commitment of those who served the first king of Israel and as his text, 'There went with him a band of men whose hearts God had touched' (1 Samuel 10:26), he set himself to conscript the souls of these young men to the allegiance of the Saviour. Finlayson had a fine sense of occasion and could always find a text and a mood to suit the need of the hour.

Returning to Hope Street Church in late 1944 his ministry there was further interrupted by duties devolving on him as Moderator of the 1945 Free Church General Assembly. Then in 1946 he demitted his charge when he was appointed to the Chair of Systematic Theology in the Free Church College, Edinburgh where he trained a whole generation of ministers before retiring in 1966 on attaining his seventieth year. In the classroom, students listened with rapt attention to his lucid and soul-warming delineation of the glorious doctrines of redeeming grace, and his services as a lecturer were constantly in demand in student circles of every kind. In such meetings he revelled in the cut and thrust of debate. Similarly on the floor of the Assembly he was a very effective debater. When his indignation was aroused he could be very crushing, on occasion excessively so, both in print and in public debate; but his ire was always given vent to in the interests of a cause and never in defence of himself personally. To those who knew him only from his reputation as a controversialist, it always came as a surprise to discover on meeting him face to face, how kind and courteous he was, a modest and a charming man, open-hearted and open-handed. He was a truly humble man who could never be persuaded to talk about himself, far less write about himself. He left no memoirs.

Undoubtedly to the general public he was first and foremost a controversialist, best known for his fiercely outspoken views ventilated in the pages of the *Monthly Record* which he edited from 1937-1958. There he did not hesitate to bring under review and evaluate against Biblical standards, the decadence which he saw emerging in all sections of society. In a day when it was not the done thing to criticise the Royals, he did not shrink from condemning members of the Royal Family for their disregard for the sanctity of the Lord's Day, warning them of the nemesis that awaited those who scorned the law of God.

He was quick to realise the all-pervasive effect which television would have on society in general and on family life in particular, and he deplored the then incipient tendency, now alas a Gaderene rush, of the BBC controllers in their programme selection to pander to the lowest common denominator in society. It was, in his view, the duty of the monopolistic BBC to maintain the Reithian maxim of giving to the general public something better, more wholesome and more uplifting than the public wanted. The spinelessness of the BBC's religious advisors was something that particularly incensed him and he was fearless in his denunciation both of the permissive opinions that were increasingly coming to the fore-front, and of the failure of church leaders to condemn what was so obviously subversive of national righteousness. For him as for the apostle Paul, there was a spirit of truth and a spirit of error; right and wrong were not meaningless abstractions and morality was not to be viewed as situation-dependent. Such outspoken-ness, although it captured the headlines, did nothing to endear him to the leaders of contemporary thought, or the framers of opinion either in the body of the church, or in the world of learning or at the seat of government. All too often his was a lone voice of protest for it was an age not just of unbelief in the world but of unbelief in the church. Like Milton's Abdiel, Finlayson held unswervingly to his convictions.

'   . . . faithful found
Among the faithless, faithful only he;
Among innumerable false, unmoved,
Unshaken, unseduced, unterrified

His loyalty he kept, his love, his zeal;
Nor number, nor example with him wrought
To swerve from truth, or change his constant mind
Though single.'

Despite his isolation from the church in the world and from its corridors of power, Finlayson was far from being a separatist. He had a catholicity of outlook that allowed him to share in fellowship with members of other Christian churches to an extent unequalled by any of his contemporaries in the Free Church of Scotland. Neither diversities of church orders nor of forms of worship inhibited him from associating with other Christians where there was a unity in the Spirit. He was prepared to make common cause with all who shared a like precious faith in the truth revealed in Scripture and who enjoyed a common experience of the grace of God in Jesus Christ. His was that true ecumenicity which belongs to the domain of faith and doctrine. Consequently he always counted it a privilege to be invited to minister the Word to Christian believers who gathered together, as at the Llandrindod Wells Convention in 1954, for the purpose of being built up in their faith.

The addresses which formed the morning Bible readings at the Convention are here reprinted in the colloquial style in which they were delivered. It is not of course in the style to which he himself, purist that he was, would have consented for a published version. The original publication was put through the press without consultation with the preacher, but we are all indebted to the vision which inspired the Convention officials at the time to make these addresses available to a wider public. The content is truly the finest of the wheat, given in good measure, heaped up, pressed down and running over. And for those of us who can cast our minds back to life's glorious morning when first we heard his preaching, what blessed memories are here evoked! What rich recollections are here called forth! We hear again the messenger of grace, and sense anew the tenderness, the earnestness, the unction with which he proclaimed the consolations of the gospel to eager hearts. The person and work of the Saviour was always to be found in the forefront of Finlayson's preaching. In the pages that follow, that mighty and mysterious work accomplished on Calvary's cross by the God, who was both creator and redeemer, is brought before us in all its greatness, with clarity, reverence and spiritual insight. In the suffering Saviour we see the holiness, the glory and the grace of the God with whom we have to do.

R A Finlayson died in Edinburgh on 19 February 1989, and his mortal remains were laid to rest in the burying ground of Lochcarron, there to await the resurrection of the just.

I R MacDonald

PART ONE

THE CREATOR AS REDEEMER

CHAPTER 1

THE CREATOR AS REDEEMER

'But if our gospel be hid, it is hid to them that are lost:
In whom the god of this world hath blinded the minds of
them which believe not, lest the light of the glorious
gospel of Christ, who is the image of God, should shine
unto them.

For we preach not ourselves, but Christ Jesus the
Lord; and ourselves your servants for Jesus' sake.

For God, who commanded the light to shine out of
darkness, hath shined in our hearts, to give the light of the
knowledge of the glory of God in the face of Jesus Christ'
(2 Corinthians 4:3-6).

It is this passage on which I would like to dwell, hoping to
gather in your thoughts around this great thing that had
happened when the Holy Spirit shone into our hearts with
the light of the knowledge of God's glory, radiant from the
face of Jesus Christ.

The situation that Paul and his fellow-workers met with at
Corinth was sad and discouraging in the extreme. But it is a
situation that has been all too familiar to the gospel
preacher since that day. The gospel was 'hid' to many in
Corinth, a closed book, a mystery impenetrable. And it was
a hid gospel for the saddest of all reasons, 'The god of this
world blinded the eyes of them that believed not'.

Here were two processes going on. They believed not, they closed their eyes to the light they had, and then the god of this world removed their sight, and now they cannot see, for the god of this world took away their vision. They refused to believe, and now they cannot believe. What use is it then, to preach to such people the gospel of Jesus Christ? What use is it to uplift Christ before the eyes of men and women who are sightless? This is a dilemma that the gospel preacher still finds himself in. He is commanded to uplift Christ in the gospel to men who have no eyes to see him, to men who cannot receive him!

Paul faced that problem in all its implications, and he fell back on God, on the God who saved him, and the God who did such great things in his own experience. That was indeed the Creator-God, the God who made the worlds, the God who brought light out of primeval darkness. He was the God who shone in their hearts and gave a new light, 'The light of the knowledge of the glory of God', and that light reached him and his fellow believers 'in the face of Jesus Christ'.

Now that is where you and I stand today. We are dealing with a Creator-God, and his creative work has been manifested in us, and we are assuredly witnesses to the fact that nothing is too hard for the Lord. We are miracles of creative and redemptive grace. Let us think together of the wondrous work of divine illumination, when God shone in our hearts with the light of the knowledge of his glory when first we met Jesus. And we are to ponder the great and glorious fact that, while once we were darkness, now we are light in the Lord, so that we may walk as children of light.

Let us consider the three great facts that we have in this passage. First of all, how did God do this great work of illumination in our hearts? Then, what kind of light did he bring to our hearts? And then, how through what medium did that light reach us? What is the firmament from which the light of divine illumination has shone upon our darkened hearts to give us new perception, new understanding, new light in the Lord?

The way of Illumination

First of all then, how has God done this great work of illumination in our hearts? It is the God who caused the light to shine out of the darkness who has shone in our hearts. Here Paul brings us back to the God of Creation, and lets us see him at work once again on a new creation, and he seems to find in the old creation an emblem and a token of the new. It may indeed be true that that is why God has given us such a clear and full account of his first creation, that we might follow his footprints, and see the Creator-God becoming the Redeeming-God in Jesus Christ. For we do believe that the first creation contains, to the spiritual eye, a blueprint of the second creation, and that if we follow the footprints of the creating God we shall see there tokens of the Saviour we have met in Jesus Christ. For we believe that the work that God has done in our hearts none but the Creator could do. We believe that it was the God of Genesis who came to work out a new creation by his own almighty power.

For here again God is at work as of old with a creative word. You remember that when the world of old was shrouded in the darkness of night, God came forth with majesty and uttered the great *fiat*, 'Let there be light!' That word was a putting forth of creative power, and it cleft, like

19

a beam of light, its way through the night; it scattered the darkness, and light dawned upon a dead and deserted world. We believe that that is precisely what God, in Jesus Christ, has done in our hearts where the darkness and deadness and desolation of death had reigned. When friends spoke to us of Jesus and asked us to look upon his pierced hands and side, we could not see, we could not understand, we were like Robert Murray McCheyne, who testified in his own experience:

> I oft read with pleasure, to soothe or engage,
> Isaiah's wild measure, and John's simple page,
> But e'en when they pictured the blood-sprinkled Tree,
> Jehovah Tsidkenu seem'd nothing to me.

That was the testimony of many souls. But in a day of grace, a word of authority came from God; it was truly a creative word, it cleft a way for itself into the night that covered our nature, and what was impossible for human power and human skill to do, God, by a word of authority, did himself. He broke our darkness, he scattered the clouds that enveloped us, and lo! the day dawned, we saw light, spiritual light, God had spoken a creative word.

And God is at work as of old in a progressive development of light. We remember that, in the first creation, light came progressively. It was not the sun in its meridian splendour that shone; indeed there is evidence that the sun had come at a much later period than the light. But the light did come, it came to wax and grow. And it is significant that at every period in God's creative work, we read, 'And the evening and the morning were the first day, the evening and the morning were the second day', and so on. Why should it be evening and morning? This is not after the manner of man's toil; he works from morning to evening. It is not enough to say that this is a Jewish division of time. We have to get behind that Jewish division of time, and ask how it came about that the Jew was taught to regard time as moving from evening to morning. It was God's pattern of workmanship. He is always facing the light, his back is on the evening, his face is towards the waxing light, and the rising sun. And if that was true in the natural creation, it is blessedly true in the spiritual creation. When God shines in our hearts with spiritual illumination, it is twilight with our souls; we see, though we see but dimly.

Yet God comes with waxing light, and as God's work develops, the light progresses until, eventually, it reaches noonday splendour. Our face is towards the sun-rising, and our souls are looking towards the meridian splendour of God's fully developed work, and of God's self-revelation to our souls. We are always going from the evening to the morning as the work of grace progresses in our souls.

We know that God is at work once again, in an ordered sequence of events, as he was in the first creation, for we know that there was a sequence in the divine operation. But the light was a harbinger of all life upon earth. As long as night had shrouded the world there was nothing on earth but desolation and death; nothing could live where the earth was enveloped in darkness; in the outer cold of space there was nothing but death. But when light came, things began to happen on earth. Not only did the clouds lift and the darkness break, and the day dawn, and the mountains of snow and ice melt, but life came with the light. The grass began to grow in the field, the trees in the forest, fish were placed in the ocean, birds in the air, beasts in the field, and eventually man came. But the light was the prerequisite of life, and the harbinger of every blessing that God was to give to the world.

In like manner, is it not true that while the darkness of nature shrouded our hearts, there was nothing there but desolation and death? As long as we are ignorant of God in Jesus Christ we are spiritually dead; there can be no life at all as long as we are estranged from God, and aliens to his life and love. But when that light shone into our hearts, then life came. It was a harbinger of every blessing; every growth and every development in our being came because the light of the knowledge of Jesus shone into our hearts.

Is it not true then, that we, who have been saved by grace, have felt the creative power of God? Is it not true that the God who laid the foundations of that first creation, and brought light out of primeval darkness, is the God who has shone into our hearts, and laid the foundations of a new creation which sin will not mar, and the flesh and the Devil cannot destroy? Yes, our dealings have been with the Creator-God who made himself known savingly and redeemingly to us in Jesus Christ his Son.

The Nature of the Illumination

And what light did God bring to our darkened hearts? It is called here, 'The light of the knowledge of the glory of God'. Let us try to examine the nature of that light. It is always difficult to examine the light. Even natural light evades investigation to a large extent. Yet we know there are several kinds of rays that blend together to make what we ordinarily call white light. Light can be broken up into its component rays, so we think God has broken up here spiritual light into three component rays.

First of all, the quality, the very nature of the divine illumination. It is God's own glory that came back to our desolate hearts. You see, that was the dignity and the honour of man in his first creation, that he was the depository of God's glory. God gave to the man he made in his image his own fellowship and his own glory. Sin came and desecrated the temple of man's nature, and God departed and took his glory away. And the fires on the altar of man's heart went out, and the temple of the human soul was left desolate, desecrated, and unclean. And that was the state of man by nature.

But when God came back in redemption, it was the divine glory that returned to the temple that had been cleansed, and to an altar on which the blood of Calvary had been sprinkled. And God returned in his glory to the desolate and darkened heart of man, for it was the life of God in the quickening of the Holy Spirit that came to us in the day of our redemption. We became partakers of the divine nature, and the uncreated glory of God returned to the temple of the human soul. That is really the nature of the light, it is the glory of God's life and God's presence and God's fellowship, that has come to us.

But here it is called the *knowledge* of the glory of God. Well, you know how little knowledge we have of natural light, how little knowledge we have of the sun in the heavens. Sometimes by means of the spectroscope, or by means of the natural spectrum we call the rainbow, we do get a glimpse of the multi-splendour and glory of the light of Nature. Yet, to a large extent, the glory of the sun is hid

23

from us. In its blazing light it is beyond our perception and our understanding. Yet an amazing thing has happened when God shone into our hearts: he gave us the knowledge of his own divine glory. He came nigh to our understanding, to our apprehensions, and our final faculties were brought into close, intimate touch with the glory of the invisible God. God in Jesus Christ came within reach of finite man. And now our whole manhood can embrace the knowledge that he has given us. Our minds can see, our consciences can interpret, our hearts can feel, our wills can respond, and our whole being can go out in loving perception and in willing apprehension of the knowledge of God's glory that he has given us. 'And this is the life eternal, that they may know thee, the only true God'. That is the wonderful thing that has happened in our redemption, that God in Christ has drawn so near that we, who are finite creatures, can behold God in Christ and say, 'We see God, we know God'. And in that knowledge of God there is life eternal.

But it is called here, '*the light* of the knowledge of the glory of God'. When knowledge becomes light, it is transmuted into a living force and a living reality. Knowledge is not always light. There is such a thing as natural knowledge, natural understanding, natural perception of the deep mysteries of nature. But that knowledge produces not one spark of light. But when we get a knowledge of the glory of God, it is knowledge that is transfused into light, knowledge that takes hold of all our faculties, and knowledge that makes use of all that God has given us, till we become 'light in the Lord'.

You remember, that is what happened in connection with the two travelling to Emmaus. Three wonderful things happened when the Stranger talked with them in the way. First, they had a *heart-emptying* experience. As they poured out their disappointment, their disillusionment, and their well-nigh despair, before the Stranger in the way, their hearts were emptied of false knowledge, of prejudice, of darkness, of misunderstanding. And then a second thing happened. There was a *heart-filling* experience, when the Lord took out of the Scriptures the things concerning himself, and made these things known to them; and enabled their understanding, with renewed vigour, to grasp the meaning of the things they heard but did not understand before, a heart-filling experience. But before he left them he did something more, he kindled that knowledge into a fire till their hearts *burned* within them. And it was the fire that brought light and energy and power and purity into their experience.

And that is what the Spirit of the living God does when he enters the darkened natures of men. He brings the glory of God nigh to us, and he empowers and re-invigorates our faculties to perceive and apprehend the glory of God who has come nigh to us, and there he makes that knowledge, not a dead perception, but a living flame. He baptises us with the Holy Ghost and with fire, and it is when that knowledge of God becomes a burning fire within us that we feel its drive and its power, its cleansing and consuming influence. Then we know the meaning of 'The light of the knowledge of the glory of God'. That is what happened when our hearts were illumined.

The Medium of Illumination

From where did that light come to us? What was the

medium through which it reached us? What was the firmament from which this sun shone? 'In the face of Jesus Christ.' What is meant by the 'face' of Jesus Christ? It is the visible appearance of Christ, the Person of Christ. Just as you say to a friend, 'I was glad to see your face', meaning, yourself, in intimate acquaintance. So the 'face' of Jesus Christ means the incarnate God, God manifested in the flesh. That is how the glory of God could become a matter of knowledge and light to us. God veiled his own glory in the manhood of Jesus Christ, and he veiled that glory not to conceal, but to reveal! And he so veiled his glory that, when those closest to him beheld him, they said, 'We beheld his glory, the glory as of the only begotten of the Father, full of grace and truth'. The Incarnation is a concealment of the glory of God, that it might be revealed to us. It was God drawing a veil over his uncreated glory, that the souls of his people might look and live, that souls might see his glory in the face of Christ and not be consumed. That is the meaning of it - in the 'face' of an *Incarnate Saviour*.

But we have seen that glory most of all in the face of a *Crucified Saviour*. When our Lord hung on the tree the sun was darkened, the natural light had been extinguished. And that impenetrable darkness of the cross has been a wonderful introduction to God for you and me. Just as when the sun undergoes a natural eclipse, the astronomer trains his telescope on the sun, and after the eclipse has passed he tells us some of the wonderful things he has discovered about the sun under the eclipse. He tells us that he has learned something new about the depth of the sun, and mysteries concerning the sun's nature and operation that he could not find out until the sun was under an eclipse.

And you and I can testify, with great sincerity, that it was in the darkness of Calvary that our souls beheld the glory of the great God, reconciling us to himself in Jesus Christ his Son. And as the eye of faith is trained upon the eclipse of Calvary, we make new discoveries of God's wonderful purpose, of God's mind and heart and will towards us. We learn concerning God, in that dense darkness of the cross, what we never would have known unless it had been mediated to us through the cross on which Jesus died. So, therefore, the 'face' of Jesus Christ is the face of a crucified Saviour.

But I wish to say that it will be eternally mediated to us through the Lamb in the midst of the throne. We believe that what is written in the Book of Revelation, 'And they shall see his face', is the crown and copestone of the Bible. We believe that if we would not see God, it would not be worth starting our journey! And it is the faith and hope and expectation of seeing him that keeps us going. And we cross the Jordan itself unafraid, because we hope to see his face at the journey's end. But it is only through a mediating Saviour. I believe it is through Jesus Christ who was crucified, through the broken manhood of the Lord of glory, that God shall mediate the knowledge of himself to us for ever and ever. 'For the Lamb that is in the midst of the throne shall lead us', and if we shall be fed and led, it is in the direction of knowing God more and more, and being filled with the light of the knowledge of his glory.

If that be true then, it is our confident expectation that though there be much darkness remaining in us, and though we feel that sin still lingers to cloud our sky, yet once we have seen his face in peace, every cloud shall lift, and we shall see God in Christ for ever mediated to our souls, in all the blessedness of his love and fellowship through Jesus Christ our Saviour. That is the firmament in which the divine illumination streams down upon our souls.

Now, if that be all true, and I do think it is, what manner of men and women ought we to be? God has done a wonderful thing for us, the Creator-God has wrought marvellously in us. When our hearts were desolate and dark, he brought a divine illumination to us. He did it with divine authority. He did it with divine skill, with divine wisdom. The God who caused the light first of all to shine out of darkness, he is the God who has shone in our hearts, and the light he gave us was his own glory; his own glory transmuted so that it might be apprehended by our quickened understanding, by our sanctified knowledge, and so apprehended in our knowledge that it became a light and fire within us; the fire was again rekindled upon the altar, and the knowledge of our God became the light of life to us. And we know, we are positively sure, that it was in the face of Jesus Christ, that that knowledge reached us.

Today, if we want to grow in grace, if we want to develop in the knowledge of God, it is only by looking to the face of Jesus Christ. You cannot grow in knowledge by looking within yourself. You may have to look within in order that you may be appalled at the darkness, you may have to look within in order that you may abhor your vileness; but your safety and your deliverance lie in looking without. And your knowledge comes from the face of Jesus Christ, as it shines upon you in intimate, loving fellowship, as you meet in Christ around his Word at the Mercy-Seat. Do then grow in grace by growing in the knowledge of your Lord and Saviour Jesus Christ.

But if there be one present of whom it is true that he or she is still sightless, who is saying, 'What can Christ mean to me?' Look to Christ!

There are men who rule God out of his universe, and who claim that God did not act as Creator. Things have happened by chance, or by an inherent force in Nature; things have evolved without the controlling, directing hand of God. And one of the most difficult things they find to explain on this principle is the creation of the eye. The eye is such an intricate mechanism, and shows such signs of skill in design and precision, that it is very difficult to believe that it could have happened by accident. But yet they try to explain it in this way. They say the creature was lying out in the sun for many millions of years, and the sun was streaming down on the skin, and it concentrated on a certain spot, and eventually there was a response in the skin to the light of the sun, and through many millions of years, the eye opened up in the skin!

If there are men who believe that, I suppose it cannot be helped! But you and I believe that here is a great spiritual fact. When you turn your blinded eye to Jesus then, in the words of the chorus you and I have learned:

Turn your eyes upon Jesus,
  Look full in his wonderful Face,
And the things of Earth will grow strangely dim,
  In the light of his glory and grace.

From Christ comes sight to sightless eyes!

PART TWO

THE CROSS
IN THE EXPERIENCE OF OUR LORD

CHAPTER I

ISAIAH'S COMPREHENSIVE VIEW

The summing-up of the passion song

Our theme for these Bible readings is the cross in the experience of our Lord, and when I ventured to give this title to our theme I was concerned with the cross as the culmination of Christ's redeeming passion, the cross as the final act of atonement for sin. Our task will to be to travel through the Gospel narratives, and especially through the last days of our Saviour's humiliation, in order to find there the factual basis of the evangelical doctrine of the atonement, which is the very heart and pith of our evangel.

We are often derided as propounding theories of the atonement which have no existence except in our own imagining; or which we have accepted unquestioningly and uncritically from a past age; or, as it is so often put, which we derive from Paul who superimposed this doctrine of the atonement on the simple narrative of Christ's life and death.

True, we acknowledge that we are debtors to Paul and to his fellow apostles for a doctrine of atonement that provides us with an adequate and complete interpretation of what happened in the sufferings and death of Jesus Christ; an interpretation without which the passion and death of our Lord would have remained largely meaningless to us, and with that key in our hands we can open doors that would have remained for us shut forever; shut to our understanding, and even to our faith. But we hold that the doctrine of the atonement found in the latter part of the New Testament in the teaching of the apostles is deeply and securely rooted in the Gospel narrative of the sufferings and death of Jesus Christ. And we will try, with the help of God's Spirit, to examine afresh the records of our Lord's suffering and death, that we may trace there these very elements that form the doctrine of a substitutionary atonement, and show these elements in relentless operation in the experience of a sin-bearing Saviour.

Now, strangely enough, I am not taking you first of all to the New Testament but to the Old, to the Prophecy of Isaiah. We, who are so accustomed to reading the New Testament page, can scarcely realise how deeply our Lord's mind was immersed in the Old Testament, how his thought and feelings were coloured and shaped by what he read there. His deepest experiences on earth were interpreted in terms of Old Testament prophecy, and found expression in Old Testament language.

When the Father spoke to him through the cleft heavens it was to employ the language of prophecy, and confirm the word spoken by psalmist and prophets. And when he himself entered into the deepest experience of humiliation and suffering it was in the mirror of Old Testament prophecy that he saw these reflected and interpreted.

And during his last days he dwelt much in the Old Testament, and its language was consistently and constantly on his lips. This is particularly true of the book of

Isaiah, and very specially of the fifty-third chapter. Again and again he directed his disciples to that chapter as affording them an insight into what was about to happen to him. When he told them of his impending death and open shame, he cushioned their minds against the shock by telling them that it stood written: 'And he was numbered with the transgressors'. And at the close of the proceedings, when the curtain falls on the shocking scene, Mark recalls that warning of Jesus, and tells us this had to happen: 'And the scripture was fulfilled which saith, And he was numbered with the transgressors'.

And out of that chapter I am choosing one passage to sum up the whole doctrine of atonement, and to place it in its true setting in the experience of our Lord. Now read the first few verses of this chapter.

It opens on a note, a questioning note, indicating wonder, perplexity, bewilderment, 'Who has believed our report?' The report given of a suffering Saviour was, in its unexpectedness, unbelievable. 'To whom is the arm of the Lord revealed?' This thing that was happening, surely the arm of Israel's God could not be discerned there! And this is the mystery - 'he shall grow up before him as a tender plant' - a sapling - 'and as a root out of the dry ground' - shrivelled and unbecoming, lifeless; 'he has no form nor comeliness, and when we shall see him there is no beauty that we should desire him. He is despised and rejected of men, a Man of Sorrows and acquainted with grief, and we hid, as it were, our faces from him, he was despised and we esteemed him not.'

Then light begins to break upon the mystery; the sufferings of the servant of Jehovah have some connection with his people's sin: 'Surely he has borne our griefs and carried our sorrows, yet we did esteem him stricken, smitten of God, and afflicted'. And then, in one wonderful passage, the prophet sums up the whole mystery of sin and suffering, of our blessedness and his anguish: 'But he was wounded for our transgressions, he was bruised for our iniquities, the chastisements of our peace was upon him, and with his stripes we are healed'.

Here we have the very heart of the Christian view of the cross, the believer's view of Jesus in his sufferings; and I have chosen it in order to put it into the Gospel narrative of Christ's sufferings and death. And we are considering it as a sort of introduction, summing up the doctrine of atonement in Christ's experience and ours, for I believe it provides us with directions, road signs and traffic lights, indicating the path our Saviour trod in the depth of his humiliation.

It is true, of course, that we cannot intellectually or morally tread the path, but faith can view the Lord descending by these steps in humiliation and death, and from these unplumbed depths faith can bring back strength and hope, and comfort for the soul. 'The heart', says Pascal, 'knows a reason which reason does not know.'

And without attempting to make unnecessary distinctions, it is clear that this verse marks four steps in the humiliation of Christ: wounded, bruised, chastised, and enduring sores or stripes. It is equally clear that it marks four steps in the soul's conviction of sin: our transgressions, our iniquities, our dispeace, our disease. And these two go together - the sense of sin and the understanding of his sufferings.

Man's Sin

And it is a view of sin and suffering that is fourfold and progressive. We travel, as it were, from the circumference to the centre. First of all, we have here a fourfold and progressive view of man's sin. Four words are used: transgressions, iniquities, dispeace, disease. There you have movement, progress in words, from the circumference of life to its very heart and centre. Sin, you see, progresses in time, and some would believe that sin does not cease to progress in time, it progresses even in eternity.

First of all it is called *transgression*. This is the most outward aspect of sin. Transgression, in the Hebrew word as in the English, signifies a stepping over, a walking across, where a man passes the boundary line, and commits an act of trespass. It is a public act of trespass. This is the outworking of sin in the *life and conduct* of man; it is an act of violence on the prerogative of God. This, you remember, was the manifestation that sin took at the first, when God placed a boundary line between his own province and man's, and man overstepped this boundary - he committed an act of trespass upon what was God's province. That is sin in the life, 'transgression'.

But further it is called *iniquities*, and the Hebrew word indicates, as the English indeed does, perversity. It gets behind transgression and signifies inequality, inequity, crookedness, perverseness. It refers to *character and spirit*, to disposition, and it depicts sin as a radical twist of disposition and spirit; a life whose ruling principle, whose inner spirit, is out of alignment with the will of God; a moral maladjustment. You see, that goes deeper than transgression; it is the root from which transgression springs. It has to do with our state in relation to law, to the will of God. It is, to use Paul's term, 'lawlessness', involving us in guilt and condemnation - 'iniquities'.

The third picture of sin here is *dispeace*, a situation in which peace would have to be restored. The absence of peace suggests the presence of dispeace, of rebellion, of enmity, of hatred. Here is sin entrenched in the heart of man, the seat of emotion and impulse. At the volitional and emotional centre of life, sin is seated as rebellion and anarchy against God.

The fourth word, the fourth picture, we have here is that of *disease* - a situation that needs healing. This is a radical and chronic condition of the *entire spiritual being* of man. Sin has infected the springs of life and sent streams of disease through the whole being. The entire spiritual life is affected, and the entire man, from the crown of the head to the soles of the feet, is sick, diseased, full of wounds and putrefying sores; there is no soundness in him.

That is the comprehensive picture of man's sin that we receive at the foot of the cross, and it deals with sin in its implications in human life and character, in the human heart and the human soul. It enables us to follow the slimy trail of sin to the centre and citadel of man's spiritual being. It is an awful exposure of human nature that we have in the cross in Jesus Christ, and before the gospel can become good news it must be accepted as bad news. It is an unmasking of the condition of the human heart, the state of the human soul, the terrible disintegration of the human personality, brought to pass by the inworking of sin in our nature.

Christ's Sufferings

Secondly, we have here a fourfold and progressive view of our Saviour's sufferings, taking us once again from the circumference to the centre, and you will see that it bears a striking resemblance to sin's nature and sin's progressiveness.

Wounded

First of all, 'he was *wounded*'. This is the outward aspect of Christ's suffering, inflicted upon him in and through the body. It indicated violence, culminating in the breaking of his manhood in death. This was the counterpart, in Christ's experience, of man's transgression, of the trespass of man's sin, for this was the supreme act of trespass. Man's assault upon the manhood of the Son of God was the supreme act of transgression. It was necessary that the storm should break in all its fury around his manhood; for in that manhood he linked himself with frail and mortal men in order that in him, the representative Man, man might make a new start, build on a new foundation, and he become the head of a new humanity. In that manhood he could and must suffer as the one who identified himself with men, and became man's surety and representative.

Thus it was that on the outward fringe of his redemptive sufferings Christ had to meet with the representatives of evil in the persons of men and devils. Sin was an act of public trespass, and his wounds must receive the same exposure and publicity as the sin that caused it. That, surely, is a sufficient explanation of the fact that 'this thing was not done in a corner'. Suffering nature asks for privacy in its hour of trial; even the animal that is wounded in the hunt leaves the herd and looks for a place of solitude where it may bleed and die alone. Suffering humanity is given the right to privacy, especially when the nature is racked in pain and breaks in death. But this privacy was denied to our Lord; he was lifted up upon a cross to die. Why? 'He was wounded for our transgressions.' Sin was a public trespass, an act in defiance of the Most High. Sin was a public rebellion against the rule of God and public sin must be met in a public way. And in that assault, his manhood, his sacred Body, was wounded.

How true this was to fact may be glimpsed in the nature and variety of the wounds inflicted upon the body of our Lord. There are, I believe, five types of wounds known to medical science: a *contused wound*, where the flesh is bruised; a *lacerated wound*, where the flesh is torn; a *penetrated wound*, where the flesh is pierced; a *perforated wound*, one that goes right through; an *incised wound*, when there is a gash made in the flesh.

Now, reverently, we look at the wounded manhood of our Lord, and find that his body bears all these wounds: a contused wound, when he was struck with the rod; a lacerated wound, when he was scourged with the cruel thong; a penetrated wound, when the thorns pierced his brow; a perforated wound, when the nails were driven through the hands and feet; and an incised wound, when the Roman spear was driven into his side.

He met with violence in every form, and nothing is more completely proved by historical evidence than this, that 'he was wounded', and that this violence involved death. In the realm of the body he died death outright - it was his last act of obedience. And there you see sin: the sin that wrought it, its cruelty, its malice, its power! There you have atonement: representation and identification, the one for the many, the second Adam as the head and surety of the new humanity, 'wounded for our transgressions'.

Bruised

He was *bruised*; and man's iniquities and Christ's bruising are brought together. Here we turn from the sin that wrought it to the sin that needed it, from man's transgression to man's guilt, from the representative man to the one to whom guilt was imputed.

This lies deeper than outward transgression. As I said, it is something of which the transgression is the fruit. It is the fact of being out of alignment with the will of God, the guilt of being lawless and rebels. Guilt is thus behind transgression; it is the parent of transgression. Now, our Lord was bruised for our iniquities. This brings us deeper into the mysteries of his sufferings when 'the Lord laid upon him the iniquity of us all'. Before, Christ was a passive sufferer, now he is active in his suffering. He is a sin-bearer.

There is evidence, for those who will look for it, that Christ was all his life long a sin-bearer; that he was ever conscious of standing in the sinner's place; that from the cradle to the grave he bore the sins of many. But it was a progressive, ever-deepening experience. His manhood, through the ministry of the Holy Spirit to him, was brought more deeply into the experience of sin-bearing. He became, daily, more conscious of the burden that he bore, he felt its load increasing, till finally it crushed and bruised his soul. Is not this the meaning of the agony, of the bloody sweat, of the inner suffering of his righteous soul? It was not an act of man; it was sin-bearing.

What was happening in that dread hour, amidst the dark shadows of Gethsemane, was what Isaiah sang of in his golden passion song some five hundred years before: 'All we like sheep have gone astray, we have turned every one to his own way, and the Lord hath laid on him the iniquity of us all'. He is here the active sufferer. God came to require of him the sacrifice that in eternal covenant he had undertaken to offer.

God asks him now to step into the position of sinbearer, and he made his soul an offering for sin, a trespass offering. There can be no trespass offering without blood, so 'it pleased the Lord to bruise him', that is to say, it was in line with the divine plan and design, that he, the sinbearer, should feel consciously in his soul the weight of that immeasurable burden, till he lay there crushed and exposed before the eye of his God, the sin-bearer and the substitute of a guilty race. 'Bruised for our iniquities.'

Chastised

But further we read of his *chastisement*. He bore the chastisement of our peace, that is to say, our dispeace led to his chastisement. Now, chastisement is a family word, a domestic discipline. There had arisen a crisis of dispeace in the family of God; man had broken the peace of the universe and became estranged, an alien and an outcast. Christ took over the headship of that family; he became the elder brother, the 'brother born for adversity'. And now the stroke of chastisement for the family must fall on him. And this takes us far in, or, as we say in Scotland, 'far ben', into the sore experience of our Lord as he deals with the Judge of all men. Now man goes into the background; the bloodthirsty Jews, the time-serving Roman judge, all his accusers, slip out of sight and God steps into the foreground. It is not the sin that wrought it, it is not the sin that needed it, that we are pondering now; but the justice that demanded it.

We proceed from representation and imputation to propitiation. Did God need propitiation? Propitiation is necessary only where there is displeasure, anger, wrath. There is wrath in God, otherwise God would not be morally active. His love to good is counter-balanced by his hatred to evil. Anger, therefore, is the other side of love in God.

So the representative and substitute of the sinner and the rebel, the sinner that created dispeace and anarchy, must meet with justice, stern and unrelenting. There can be no favourites with heaven when justice is being meted out. And so the representative was struck by the rod of chastisement. Can we understand a thousandth part of what it meant for the heart of a beloved Son to be so stricken? If he felt the taunts and mockery of men till he could cry, 'Reproach hath broken my heart', even when the witness of his soul testified to his innocence, how much more was he hurt by the imputation of his God! The imputations of men could be denied and repudiated, but the imputation of God must be accepted as his portion. True, the sin imputed to him was not his own, and he could never know self-accusation, or remorse, or despair. Remember this when you sing 'In every pang that rends the heart, the Man of Sorrows had a part'.

But the agent in that affliction was his Father, now his Judge. When God, through Zechariah, gave the command to the sword to awake, the sword that gleamed of old outside the gate of a Lost Paradise, it was Jehovah himself who answered: 'I will smite the shepherd'. He, the final exactor of justice, takes the sword, as it were, out of the hands of the underlings who had wounded him, and he struck the righteous soul of the one that was his fellow and his equal. And this fact that the just exactor is the Father adds pain and anguish unspeakable to the blow, and as he reels under the shock, he cries in agony of dismay, 'My God, my God, why hast thou forsaken me?' 'He was chastised for our peace.'

Chastisement is a strong word here, but an appropriate word when dealing with truants and rebels. It gives a new penetration into the sufferings of our Lord. He endured the chastisement for the family; he met with the criminality of sin, not only of guilt, but high treason against the throne of God.

When the first Adam had sinned, God broke the silence by the cry, 'Where art thou?' There was no response from man. Man's voice was stifled by guilt and shame; and as the long, silent years had passed into centuries and millenniums, still man found no voice, no plea, no sponsor, no intercessor.

The second Adam took up the case for man. He heard the call of God, and he found a voice with which to respond. And in responding he was bringing the truant and the exile back, but at a price - that he himself must be deserted and forsaken! And the cry in Eden of old found its echo on Calvary, and its response in the anguish of his soul, 'My God, my God, why hast thou forsaken me?' That was man brought back in the agony and chastisement of the second Adam, the Lord from heaven.

So he had to stay out the storm, and his will to sacrifice was not weakened. Under his active sufferings there was his passive obedience. He turned not back till he could say: 'I restored that which I took not away'. 'He was chastised for our peace.'

Now the peace of reconciliation flows to us from God. It is indeed the peace of God into which we are lifted and it passeth all our understanding; it transcends human calculations, it contradicts human circumstances, it belies human expectations, just because it is the peace of God. But it flows ever and always from the divine reconciliation effected through the chastisement of the second Adam. In the heart of the storm he offered that peace to others, as he did to the three disciples in Gethsemane and to the malefactor on the tree.

For he is our peace who has reconciled us to God by his cross.

CHAPTER 2

THE TWO FEASTS

A Preview of the Cross

Our theme is the cross in the experience of our Lord. We are concerned with the cross as the great consummation of the work of atonement for a world's sin. We have traced in bold outline the framework of atonement in Isaiah's prophetic vision of human sin and divine suffering and soul-healing. We traced it from the circumference to the centre, from its outer reaches to its impenetrable heart.

Sin, in its outer aspect, was an open transgression, an act of public trespass. And so the cross in its outward aspect was an act of violence, the supreme act of violence. The conflict between God and sin was brought into the open, and the Son of God was wounded in the conflict. And 'he was wounded for our transgressions'.

Let us go into the Gospel narrative for the factual basis of this view of the atonement. And we find it in the consciousness of the Church, and in the self-consciousness of the Lord himself. It is the violence that found its final manifestation in his broken body that we meet with here. Christ anticipated this violence; he spoke of it again and again. To Nicodemus he spoke of himself as the impaled serpent. To the Jews he spoke of the destroying of the temple of his body, of forcibly pulling it down. To the

Greeks - or to the Greeks through Philip - he spoke of himself as the corn of wheat that must fall into the ground and there die that its hidden life may be released.

It is the same aspect of his death that we have portrayed in these two events - the supper in the home of Bethany and the supper in the upper room. They are clearly related, not only in time, but also in significance, and Christ is the centre of both. While it was true that throughout the whole of his earthly pilgrimage Christ was presented to the world as Saviour, the unveiling of his priesthood and death became more insistent and more complete in the closing scenes of his earthly life. He willed that it should be so, and he related all that was happening to his death, to that grand consummation to which he was hastening. So these two suppers shed light, each from its own angle, upon his death.

Our Supper

This is the name by which we designate the supper in the Home at Bethany. Some think that the Church of all ages was represented there. Martha - the Church serving; Mary - the Church worshipping; Lazarus - the Church risen. If indeed it be so, it is noteworthy that Lazarus - the Church in resurrection - seated with the Lord at the table, was an object of wonder. The Church is - not yet - an object of admiring wonder to the world. But the Church is meant to be a fragrance in the world, as the fragrance of Mary's anointing filled the whole house. But it is the Church worshipping at the foot of the cross that sheds this fragrance. This is indeed New Testament worship - the adoration and gratitude of a Church who is conscious that she has been redeemed by Christ's blood.

It is the Church worshipping that gets the deepest insight into the significance of the cross. How much did Mary understand of this act of redemption when she offered the fragrance of her worship? Was it a sudden and spontaneous impulse? Or was it a deliberate plan? Christ interprets it in one particular way: 'Against my burial has she done this'. Did Mary have this clear-sighted understanding of what she was doing? Did she even have a premonition of what was impending? We cannot say. The saints do more than they can understand; and they understand more than they can express. It was Pascal who said, 'The heart knows a reason which reason does not know'.

Especially is this so in the exercise of worship. Mary doubtless had the instinct, the intuition, the spiritual insight and discernment that prompted her to do this and that guided her in the doing of it. She may not have been able to express it in language - not in a way to satisfy the calculating ones who assessed the material value and complained of the 'waste'. But Mary acted on a deep-seated and sure impulse. She took the 'box' of ointment; it was a vase with a long and narrow outlet, and the contents were usually dispensed by means of a long handled spoon. On this occasion Mary acted in a manner that may not tone in with her accepted disposition as gentle, and tender of heart and hand; she took the vase and broke it.

This smashing of the vase bore to our Lord its own message; it spoke of the broken body. And accordingly he rose in her defence when the complaint was made: 'Why this waste?' His words are significant: 'Why trouble ye her?', or more accurately 'Why confuse her?' It is as if he had said: 'She has a clear spiritual conception of what she is doing; do not confuse her by cold, calculating, precise questioning of what it means.' To Judas it was an extravagance; to Mary it was an extravagance befitting his death. The vase broken to release its costly fragrance was a fitting symbol of the breaking of his sacred Manhood in order that the grace of redemption might flow to sinners of mankind.

But it is a gospel that tells of Jesus and not merely of Mary: 'Against my burying has she done this.' He received it gladly, gratefully. It strengthened him for the priestly functions on which he was entering. It marked him off as the bearer of the priestly office. In the violent breaking of the box he saw his own body broken for his people. In the pouring of the oil he read the mandate of his Church, sending him forward to do business with God on her behalf. By the Father he had been anointed in secret - anointed by the Spirit without measure - and the fragrance of that anointing never left him. Now at the hand of Mary he was anointed by his Church, visibly and publicly. Did it mean much to him? 'When thou shalt make his soul an offering for sin, he shall see his seed.'

What does our Lord do with Mary's ointment? He accepts it gratefully - and then pours it back upon the hand that anointed him: 'Verily I say unto you, wheresoever this gospel shall be preached throughout the whole world, this also that she has done shall be spoken of as a memorial of her.' In his anointing he anointed in turn his Church, which is his body.

It is significant that the only one who dissented and disassociated himself from this anointing - this symbolic setting apart of Christ by the Church for his priestly office - was Judas. He had no part or lot in this matter. So he took action on it that served to fulfil the symbol - he proceeded to the betrayal. As for the rest of us we gladly fall behind Mary. We see here what Christ saw - a preview of his attendance at the altar of sacrifice for the Church. We have here the deed of faith and obedience of love that become each one of us, as, in the secret of our hearts, we set him apart to be our Sacrifice, our High Priest, and our Altar.

His Supper

When we turn to the other Supper - his Supper - you will find that everything is in his hands: it is all his plan and execution. It is evidently the result of loving and careful forethought. It was deeply purposeful. He longed for it: 'With desire I have desired to eat this Passover with you before I suffer.'

The arrangements, as you will see, are in his hands. He sees to it that all the customary arrangements are made and that the Passover is observed in the letter of the law as well as in the spirit. The Old Covenant cannot go out till the New is ready to come in. So the Passover cannot go out till the Supper comes in. But the Old is the preparation of the New. The Passover of the Old Testament is thus a preparation for the Supper of the New Testament. But it is not till the Old is fulfilled that the New is born. And the Old prepares the way for the New. Consistently with this we see that the Passover provides the very setting for the Supper. If this is indeed the gospel of the New Testament reaching its birth-hour, then, as some one has put it, 'The birth-chamber is prepared by the law of the Old Covenant'.

The Passover merges into the Supper, as the stars of night fade into the light of day.

The Passover

Though it is very difficult for us to arrive at a definite conclusion as to the precise order of events that constituted the Jewish Passover at any time of its history, and more especially at the time of our Lord, it is thought that there were four cups of wine generally used, each associated with one of the benefits bestowed on Israel in its deliverance from Egypt.

The first was the *Cup of Consecration*, associated with liberty, the overall blessing involved in the Divine intervention on that night in Egypt, and pledging Israel to be the Lord's emancipated people.

The second cup was the *Showing Forth* and was accompanied by a narration of the events that led to the release from Egypt. For this reason it has often been referred to as the *Cup of Release*.

The third cup was referred to as the *Cup of Blessing*, also called the *Cup of Redemption* because it signified the complete and eternal redemption of the enslaved race.

The last cup was the *Cup of Joy*, also called the *Cup of Election*, portraying God's choice of a people. In later times it came to be called the *Cup of the Messiah*. Though it was filled and passed round, the participants did not drink of it. It betokened the Divine promise of the Messiah, but until the Messiah should come it was to be filled but not drunk, a silent reminder of the promise not yet fulfilled.

In addition there was placed on the table, cakes of unleavened bread, sauce, bitter herbs, and the Paschal lamb roasted, often referred to as 'the body' to distinguish it from the mere accessories.

We must now attempt to relate all this to what is recorded in the five records of the events in the Upper Room on the night on which our Lord was betrayed. It is exceedingly difficult to attempt a reconstruction of the Passover and the Last Supper, and some of the details I am submitting are conjectural, though in no instance, as far as I understand it, a violation of the Gospel narrative.

Jesus took, first of all, the *Cup of Consecration*, saying: 'With desire I have desired to eat this Passover with you before I suffer' (Luke 22:15). Jesus thus directed attention to himself as the central figure in the ritual, and to his coming sufferings as that which should supersede and fulfil that which happened in Egypt. This was the great divine intervention - his death.

Water, as was customary, was now brought in and Jesus rises from the table, girds himself with a towel, and sets about washing the disciples' feet. Thus he revealed himself as 'he that serves', and he taught the need of a cleansed walk.

The table is now set with bitter herbs, sauce, and the Paschal lamb, and Jesus says, 'Verily I say unto you, that one of you that eateth with me shall betray me' (Mark 14:18). This was truly the 'bitter herbs' at the feast for the Master who, 'having loved his own who were in the world loved them unto the end'.

The bitter herbs were now eaten, Judas dipping into the common sauce dish. To the repeated inquiry of the disciples, 'Is it I?', Jesus answered, 'It is one of the twelve which dippeth with me in the dish' (Mark 14:20).

The second cup, the *Showing Forth*, was passed around and Jesus began to talk, not about the Exodus from Egypt, but about his own sufferings, betrayal and death. At this stage he identified the traitor as the one to whom he should give the sop.

The bread was then broken, and the sop, after it had been dipped in the sauce, was handed to Judas, with the words, 'That thou doest, do quickly' (John 13:27). It was customary for the host at the Passover meal to do this service to any guest of the family who was present at the Passover meal, and Judas was thus branded as the 'stranger' at the meal. Though the Eleven apparently failed to grasp the significance of it, Judas himself did not. And he went out into the night!

The Paschal lamb - the body - was now eaten. It is not clear whether the third cup - the *Cup of Blessing* - was passed round. While there is nothing in the narrative to indicate that it was, there is nothing to assure us that it wasn't.

The Lord's Supper

It was at this stage that the utterly unexpected happened. Jesus, with infinite majesty and quiet deliberation, lays, as it were, the Paschal lamb aside, and places himself on the table!

He took bread again, and, having given thanks, he broke it and offered it to them saying, 'Take, eat, this is my body' (Mark 14:22). If, indeed, the Paschal lamb was commonly referred to as 'the body', did Christ's words not simply mean, 'This is my Paschal lamb', signifying that he was the Paschal Lamb in this new ordinance? This would connect the Lord's Supper with the Passover of the Old Testament as substance is connected with symbol, antitype with type. How much this understanding would have saved of wrangling and dissension over transubstantiation, consubstantiation, the Real Presence, and the rest!

Our Lord then took the cup, and history turned from

the Old Covenant to the New as he uttered the words, 'This cup is the New Testament in my blood, which is shed for you' (Luke 22:20). If we can assume that this was indeed the fourth cup, the *Cup of the Messiah*, which remained undrunk till the Messiah should come, how significant the words, 'Drink ye all of it'! (Matthew 26:27). 'You need wait no longer; the Messiah is here!' The Jews call it the *Cup of Joy* and he, too, spoke of 'My joy'.

Thus the Supper betokened the utter and complete fulfilment of all that the Passover offered and promised. On that dread night in Egypt the Passover was observed as a stay of execution of the sentence of death on the first-born; that was all, a stay of execution, till the day of God's judgment and retribution should come. Now it has arrived and there can be a stay of execution no longer. The First-born is here and he must come under the avenging stroke. The blood that availed for the first-born of Israel avails not for him. There is now no 'passing over', for he is himself the First-born of the new family of God. He is the Lamb that gives shelter, but for himself there can be no shelter when the Angel of Retribution visits the earth. And so he says tenderly, firmly, 'My body broken for you... my blood shed for you'.

And the Supper is a permanent channel by which the blessings of the grace of atonement reach us. Do not reduce it to a mere act of remembrance. He is not here as a man amongst men asking for a memorial to be set up. Men who know that death will rob them of their office try to keep some vestige of their life alive. But it is not so in his case. He wants to continue ministering his grace to the world and he does it through the emblems of his broken body and shed blood. Remembering him thus in his death brings us into the fellowship of his sufferings that we may be conformable unto his death.

Thus it is, then, that in the two Suppers we have a preview of Christ's death from two aspects - that of his Church and that of his own consciousness. In both it is a priestly sacrifice we see and a priestly function we are directed to. In both it is a *breaking*, an act of violence that releases the fragrance and the grace. In both we have a banquet of mercy and grace. Christ in his death a feast for famishing souls; life through him and life in him that there may be life for him. 'For he was *wounded* for our transgressions.'

CHAPTER 3

THE CUP AND THE CONFLICT

A Foretaste of the Cross

We believe that Christ on the cross completed a work of atonement for man's sin. We believe that in that atonement there are distinguishable elements, principles of justice and mercy, of love and grace, that operate and that determine the fullness of blessing that flows to us from the atonement. The bringing together of these principles constitutes a theory of the atonement. We think we find in the Gospel records of the sufferings and death of our Lord, a factual basis for the evangelical conception of a substitutionary atonement. We believe indeed that there is a close connection, and a striking correspondence, an indissoluble tie, between our sins and Christ's sufferings; that he was wounded for our transgressions, he was bruised for our iniquities, he was chastised because of our dispeace and that with his sores our disease may be healed.

Our theme, for that reason, is 'The Cross in the Experience of our Lord'. And by the cross, of course, we mean the climax and consummation of that work of atonement by which he made an end of sin and brought in an everlasting righteousness. In our first reading we pondered on the meaning of the atonement in Christ's experience, as Isaiah presented it to us in that great pregnant declaration: 'But he was wounded'.

And from there, we travelled to the Gospel narrative to find in the experience of our Lord, the basis for the atonement. We studied the Two Suppers, that in the home of Bethany, and that in the upper room, and we thought we saw in this a clear preview of the atonement from two angles; that of the consciousness of the Church, as represented by Mary, and that of the self-consciousness of Jesus himself. The aspect of the atonement we saw there was the breaking of the manhood of the Master in suffering and death, or, to use again the words of Isaiah, 'he was wounded for our transgressions'. He, the Son of Man, as well as the Son of God, took up the conflict for man where it had been waged and lost. He took the field again as man's representative, as the second Adam, and he was wounded unto death.

But Isaiah also saw him in prophetic vision, 'bruised for our iniquities', crushed under our guilt. There is only one way conceivable to us in which guilt can be borne by a guiltless one, and that is by imputation. The imputation of sin we cannot understand, because there is no exact parallel to it in human experience or in human relationships. But we do know in Christian experience the imputation of righteousness, and that sheds a flood of light for us on the imputation of sin. The imputation of guilt to the guiltless one can be investigated only on the side of redemption. 'He was bruised for our guiltiness.' And to get a solid foundation for this doctrine we go to the experience of our Lord in the garden of Gethsemane, and bear in mind in particular, Luke 22:39-46. Here you have a foretaste of the cross. Here you have the Cup and the Conflict.

The Two Suppers were a preview of the cross for him,

and, through his interpretation, to his disciples also, and through them to us. But there was no remaining at a distance: 'Arise let us go hence', were the words with which he left the upper room and stepped out into the night. There was nothing arbitrary or improvised about his movements these last days. He trod the path of obedience as one who had a clear-sighted understanding of the programme that was unfolding.

On this occasion his destination was the Garden, a place to which he had frequently resorted for communion and refreshment. But this time it was to be the place of conflict, the place where he should have not only a preview, but a foretaste of the cross. This was something closer, more intimate, more distressing, than he had hitherto experienced. And in approaching this solemn study we must tread reverently and cautiously.

Gethsemane is not a field for intellect, it is a sanctuary for faith. *There* was transacted something that brings us completely out of our depth, yet something that has such a distinct bearing on our redemption that we dare not pass it by. Here, in the innerness of his own experience, Christ knows what it is to be identified with the sinner, and to become himself the sin-bearer.

It can be said that Gethsemane is for us quite a new introduction to our Lord. We recognise him readily at the supper table in the upper room, where everything is calm, serene, untroubled; but from the calm serenity of the upper room, he plunged suddenly into the gloom and storm of Gethsemane, and the contrast is impressive. In the upper room you have a figure of composure and of singular spiritual strength; in the Garden you have a broken man, distressed, in anguish, conscious of his weakness, pleading for the sympathy and the vigil of three disciples. What has happened? Just this, that he was entering more consciously into the full implications of his priestly office, and of his position as sin-bearer.

And there appears indeed a gradation, a progressive deterioration, in his condition. These are the comments that we read from the Evangelists: Matthew and Mark tell us, 'he began to be very heavy', then Matthew and Mark again say, 'he began to be sorrowful'; but Mark says, 'he began to be sore *amazed*'. That word is very strong, 'a *paralysing amazement* gripped him'. Moffatt puts it, 'He began to be *appalled and agitated*'. Then in Matthew and Mark we read again that 'his soul was exceedingly sorrowful unto death'. And in Luke we read, 'And being in an agony'. This suggests that he came to realise in ever-deepening consciousness what it was to have a world's sin laid to his charge. The fact that they were the sins of those he loved dearly only added to the amazement. What a disclosure it was to him of the condition of those he loved!

Ingredients in his Cup

We have certain stepping-stones as it were, by which we may traverse through the dark, sombre shadows of Gethsemane and view something of the anguish of our blessed Lord.

Isolation

First of all, see it in *his isolation*. He separated himself first from the eight whom he left outside, and then he separated himself from the chosen three. 'He went,' Luke says, 'a stone's cast from them'. That was the physical distance - some thirty yards - but the moral and spiritual distance was immense. The distance in his own experience was infinite. It is obvious that he calmly and deliberately separated himself from his brethren at this hour. He willed that there should be this distance between them and him, between them and the place of his anguish.

But they made the distance greater, they fell asleep. 'The flesh is weak' was his own kind interpretation. There are some things that are too much for human flesh to bear, and proximity to the place of sin-bearing is one of these. There are some experiences that mere human nature cannot look into - bearing a world's guilt is one of them. Even at that distance the atmosphere, charged with terrible spiritual realities, was too oppressive and too overpowering for frail mortals, and they found refuge in sleep. Human nature retreated from the scene. They could not comprehend what was happening there. It was of a different world-order from anything within their human experience, and so the burden was borne and the conflict waged without us, without even our watching. He was completely and absolutely alone. He separated himself from his brethren.

Fear

And there was *fear in it*. I hope nobody thinks that there is anything derogatory in this - in our Lord being afraid of the Cup that passed before him at this hour; that is, of being identified with the sin he bore. Natural fear was awakened, though his courage and faith were not shaken. The desire to escape the bitter dregs of the Cup was natural. Because he was human and had a reasonable soul he shrank from bitterness so terrible. Because he was holy he desired to escape from a burden that was so loathsome, for he was now to be clothed in filthy garments. Because he was a devoted Son, he shrank with a holy sensitiveness from the prospect of his Father's sore displeasure. He had an overwhelming sense of what was impending, the agony of the cross had projected itself into his inmost experience. He already saw the Cup in all its bitterness pass before him, and he had a foretaste of it in his soul.

Weakness

Then there was his *weakness*. He stood in need of strengthening from without. Luke tells us, 'There appeared an angel unto him from heaven strengthening him'. It is obvious that under the strain his human nature was breaking. Help was rushed to him from heaven. It is clear the finger of the Father was upon the pulse of the lonely Sufferer in Gethsemane, and when the heartbeats of the One in conflict seemed to weaken, heaven concerned itself about him, and an angel was commissioned to hasten to his physical aid. It was surely a message from Home to comfort him.

We all know what it is, who have been in a foreign land, and feel the wide distance between us and kindred spirits, to get a letter from home. And here our Lord was in alien land, land utterly foreign to his righteous soul. And he was absolutely, completely alone. But there was a message from Home, telling him that heaven was behind him, the Father was with him, and all the inhabitants of glory were 'peering down' (for those are Peter's words), peering down to see what was happening.

How did the angel strengthen him? We cannot tell.

Some think the angel fell down and worshipped him, and that by the worship of the angel the glory of his divine person was presented to his human mind. To be worshipped in the nadir of his humiliation while he was struggling in the dust under the burden would no doubt be strengthening; a fore-gleam of the glory beyond Gethsemane and Calvary when angels and principalities and powers should bow the knee to him and call him Lord.

However it happened, his human nature needed strengthening, and reinforcements came from the Home above - 'an angel appeared unto him to strengthen him'.

There was a singular Christian in Scotland in the last century, Dr. John Duncan, a scholar and a saint, but best known to Scottish readers as 'Rabbi Duncan'. He had many quaint sayings to his credit, and he had this one. 'If', he said 'I arrive in glory' (and that saint always had an 'if' somewhere!); 'if', he said, 'I arrive in glory, first I shall look for the face of my Lord, and then I shall enquire for the angel that came to help my Lord in the hour of his agony in Gethsemane.' 'There appeared unto him an angel to strengthen him.'

Sweat

Then the next evidence that we have of the conflict was in the *sweat*. Luke says, 'To strengthen him', that is, to reinforce his manhood to enable him to endure the full burden of the crushing load. For it was immediately after the angel had strengthened him, that Luke recalls: 'He did sweat, as it were great drops of blood', or, as Moffatt puts it, 'His sweat fell to the ground like clots of blood'.

We are not called upon to enter into the physical or

physiological significance of this, but the Holy Spirit has noted the fact for our edification, and Luke, the beloved physician, was the one fitted to preserve the record and convey it to us. He did sweat, that is significant that he should sweat at all. It was a cold night, for even the soldiers in the open Court had made a fire of coals to warm themselves. It was a cold night, and there he lay amidst the dark shadows of Gethsemane in the open, and he did sweat. And the sweat appeared as 'drops of blood'.

So the experience involved the expenditure of no ordinary energy; and the bloody sweat suggested that it was extraordinary pressure from within. At Calvary blood was expelled from his body from without, in Gethsemane the pressure came from within. This was supremely an internal agony of soul, the other was external physical affliction. The one at Calvary was done by human weapons rupturing his arteries from without. Here was no human hand laid upon him; it was the forces of the invisible world that he was wrestling against. And remember, he had an infinite capacity for pain. We must remember that the capacity for suffering on the part of our Lord was on as high a level as was his passion from ours. The limitations imposed upon us by time and space had, at that hour, no validity for him. True, he suffered in time and space, but they were the sufferings of an infinite person who can sustain an infinite burden.

In human sufferings there are ameliorating aspects that come in by way of contrast: 'Our light affliction, which is but for a moment, worketh for us a more exceeding and eternal weight of glory'. But there were no such contrasts in the case of our Lord's sufferings. No greater or lesser. He was dealing with ultimates and with infinitudes. Infinite guilt and infinite redemption were in the scale, and he, the Holy One, had an infinite capacity for suffering.

Submission

Then there was *his acceptance of the Cup*: 'Not as I will, but as thou wilt'. With a sense of horror at the disclosure of the innerness of sin-bearing, there flashed into his soul the light of the knowledge of the Father's will; a flashback, as someone has put it, a flashback from the Councils of Eternity.

The Council of Peace, where he undertook to stand surety for the lost, became clearly visible to his eye now. That plan which he had undertaken in the tranquillity of heaven, on which he had embarked in the fullness of time, he will now see through to the end. He will drink the Cup to its bitterest dregs, and that Cup was put into his hands by a Father's hand. That for him was enough.

Remember, there was now to come into operation a Law higher than that between Father and Son. He was now the servant of Jehovah, to fulfil his will, and to execute his eternal plan. He was now the sin-bearer to meet the Judge of all men, and the Avenger of all sin. So he put his Will into his Father's hand, the willing Servant as well as the Fellow of Jehovah, the Shepherd over the flock.

Compassion

Look, lastly, at his *considerateness* for his disciples, 'Sleep on now, and take your rest,' he said. There is no trace of irony or irritation of any kind in this, need I say; they are the words of a Shepherd as he stands watch over his flock; the words of the Elder Brother who is assuming responsibility for his weaker brethren. He who knew what was in store for himself, knew also what was in store for them, and he pitied them in their frailty. They needed all the resources of energy they could lay by for the ordeal that was now ahead of them. As for himself, he set his face like a flint, and he went out to meet not what was his fate but his choice, not his misfortune but his deed. 'No man taketh it from me, I lay it down of myself, I have power to lay it down'. It was a Father's Cup put in his hands from a Father's hand, and he baptised himself to the task; that was his own word - a 'baptism' - his voluntary consecration to the ordeal and the task ahead of him.

It was thus an experience of the imputation of sin, that should bruise his righteous soul. Imputation of sin, as I have already suggested, is a mystery we cannot penetrate, because, as I said, there is no parallel to it in the sphere of human relationships. But I also suggested that there is also a glorious counterpart to it in imputed righteousness. It is from a personal experience of imputed righteousness, of pardon and reconciliation and acceptance in Christ, that we can approach and investigate this mystery.

There is a strange idea among the Scottish people that when you find a loch nestling at the foot of the high hills, that the loch is as deep as the hill at whose foot it nestles is high; that if you scale the mountain and plumb the depth of the loch, then they measure the same. That is probably a fancy, but I do know that this is a reality: the mountain of God's grace rises sheer from the ocean of Emmanuel's suffering and sorrow. And they measure the same. And it is only from the heights of God's redemption that you can know anything of the depth of a Saviour's sorrow and travail as he bore our sins in his own human consciousness right up to the tree. It is only when we have put on the Lord Jesus Christ and are clothed in his righteousness that we can understand, in any measure whatsoever, what was meant by that mysterious transaction between Father and Son: 'And the Lord laid upon him the iniquity of us all'.

But that is not the whole of the story. The beginning of it, as Isaiah pondered it and saw it, was this, 'All we like sheep have gone astray; we have turned every one to his own way'; and then, 'The Lord laid on him the iniquity of us all'. There you've got the two 'alls', like gateways, one at the beginning and one at the end, and one opens inwards and the other opens outwards. One is the entrance, and the other is the exit. They do not open in the opposite direction.

The gate by which you go in is this, 'All we like sheep have gone astray'. The first 'all' opens inwards into our sinnership, into confession and conviction, and penitence; 'like sheep' - it is collective sin, you can call it original sin if you like; but there is also personal iniquity, for 'we have turned each one to his own way'. Sin becomes personal, deeply personal - the only thing in the Universe that truly belongs to you, and the only thing that neither death nor hell can sever from you. The only thing that you can call your very own is your sin, as you see it there.

But thanks be to God, there is an exit, there is a door that swings outward into liberty and peace and acceptance through the sin-bearer: 'And the Lord hath laid on him the iniquity of us all'. Through the sin-bearer you go out from the valley of Condemnation into the sunlit uplands of God's favour and fellowship.

Don't try, I beseech you, to reverse God's order. Don't

deal with the Saviour till you know you're a sinner, for you'll never appreciate Christ, you'll never understand him. And that is the difficulty with so many; in the perversion of their nature they are wanting to go in by the door by which God asked them to come out.

You go in by the door of sinnership, accept your own condition as involved in universal sin, accept your personal responsibility as having turned to your own way, and in defiance of God chosen your way and rejected his. Then, when sin has been made personal, Christ will be personal to you, and you will find, as the prophet Isaiah put it, 'And the Lord hath laid on him the iniquity of *every one of us*', as the Welsh, the Gaelic, and the Hebrew Bible renders it. It was personal sin that was laid upon a personal Saviour; and that day you meet him, you'll see no sin but your own.

What then is your link with the Saviour? Don't talk to me about the beauty of his teaching, don't talk to me about the wonder of his miracles, or about the sanctity of his manhood; that doesn't link me to him. I have only one contact with this Lord, it's the sin he bore. 'Tis my sin, 'tis my sin and only mine; 'twas my burden, 'twas my sin, and so I look upon him whom I pierced, and the gates of penitence are opened and I mourn; I mourn as a mother mourns for her first-born. What a personal grief! Is there a mother here that lost her first-born? Oh! What a personal grief as a parent mourns for an only child. And as I look upon him whom I pierced, I mourn as a parent mourns for an only son, and as a mother mourns for her first-born child. There, sin becomes personal, and the Saviour becomes as personal as sin, and you and he meet together, for you are the sinner that he came to save.

CHAPTER 4

THE LAMB FOR THE SACRIFICE

Christ before his Examiners

We are viewing the cross as the final act of atonement. From the cradle to the grave Jesus bore the sins of many, but he was entering more deeply in his consciousness into the implications of sin-bearing. He was experiencing more and more what it meant to be surety for a world's sin.

Sin was transgression, an act of trespass that manifested itself against the earthly manhood of the Son of God - and 'he was wounded'. Sin was a burden of guilt that must be borne, and it was a crushing experience to which Gethsemane is an introduction. Sin was dispeace, and the conscience that bore witness to transgression in the outer life, to perversity in the human spirit, must now pursue its witness to the ravages of sin within the heart at the emotional and volitional centre of life. There it was dispeace, disorder, rebellion, anarchy, enmity, hatred, complete aversion to God. It is obvious that a work of atonement must reckon with heart-enmity and discord God-wards. It must reckon with it, and make propitiation. Propitiation, first God-wards, and then man-wards; peace with God, and then peace within.

We believe that our Lord Jesus Christ brought into the open the hatred to God, the aversion to God, that dwelt in the human heart. But we believe that its outer aspects in his condemnation before the Tribunal of Earth had its counterpart and its reality God-ward, in an inner reality in which he stood before the Bar of his God, condemned in our stead, himself without blemish, yet the Lamb for our Sacrifice.

Let us ponder then together, this matter of the arrest and trial and condemnation of our Lord, as he stood, the sinbearer for the sinner, making propitiation for sin that was not his own, restoring that which he took not away. This, perhaps, is the most difficult aspect of our Lord's sufferings. It is a subject that is difficult to handle, and very difficult to present in brief compass, and I therefore crave your patience as we go together through this passage.

The Arrest

First of all, we shall look at the historical fact of his arrest and trial. There were two incidents that helped the rulers to make up their minds that Jesus must be got out of the way. They were the cleansing of the Temple and the raising of Lazarus. The Sadducees were the party then in power; and the raising of Lazarus was particularly offensive to them since they professed disbelief in the resurrection or the future life; and the cleansing of the Temple from its unholy traffic affected them financially, for much of their revenue was derived from that source.

So there were theological and financial reasons wedded together, not for the first time or the last, for which Jesus must be silenced, and, if possible, removed. But they wished to avoid the Passover as the occasion. The crowds were entering Jerusalem from the provinces; many of them had shown deep interest in Jesus, and were enquiring,

'What think ye, will he come up to the Feast?' So the rulers decided, 'not on the Feast Day, lest there be an uproar among the people'. But Judas intervened unexpectedly. When he came forward with his plan for the betrayal, the arrest was simplified considerably, and it was too good an offer to let slip. So the rulers decided to act on the instigation of Judas.

The warrant for the arrest of Jesus was no doubt signed by the High Priest, the President of the Sanhedrin, and it was carried out by the Temple Guard, a body of Jewish retainers or officials that did service in the Temple Courts. And our Lord surrendered immediately to their warrant; significant that he recognised the authority of the rulers of his people.

Judas stood by, an amazed beholder. How foolish and futile his treachery now seemed. How contemptible his advice to the soldiers, 'Whomsoever I will kiss, the same is he; hold him fast'. 'Come ye out as against a thief with swords and staves?' asked Jesus. No, this was not a forcible arrest, this was a voluntary self-surrender by one who was in full control of the situation. How foolish even was the action of Simon who drew a sword and cut off the servant's ear. How feeble his sword was when placed alongside the twelve legions of angels which his Master had then at his command. How little any of them understood the majesty of the Lord's self-giving.

On the part of Jesus there was no sense of coercion. It was a voluntary surrender; he stepped forward with the words, 'Whom seek ye?' and at once he yielded himself to their wile. And so Jesus left himself in the hands of violent men. There were no restraints now. It was man's hour, and man was allowed to give full vent to the instincts of his depraved nature. Heaven seemed to withdraw even the restraints of common grace, decency, humaneness and compassion; those things that lift a man above the brute and the devil seemed withdrawn. Man is in the ascendancy, and the Son of Man is in chains. Man comes to the forefront and God, as it were, steps into the background. The earthly judge begins to play his role, and he does it openly. The conflict that was carried on in secret in Gethsemane is now brought into the open, and carried on openly in the world's tribunals. The Lamb of God comes under the judgment of men, men whose authority to judge is given them of God.

Under Scrutiny

Let us look, first of all, at the Lamb under scrutiny - Christ before his examiners. It was the Passover Week and every Jewish family had secured its Paschal lamb. The lamb in each case was presented to the priest of the Temple, that it might be examined and certified 'without spot or blemish', that is, perfect outwardly and sound inwardly. One of the priests, with the help of his assistants, made the scrutiny, and when the lamb was pronounced free from injury and blemish it was handed back for the Passover Feast.

It is significant, we shall not put it higher than that, significant, that about the time the Paschal lambs were receiving the scrutiny from the priesthood, Jesus was actually entering Jerusalem to undergo his trial, and come under the scrutiny of his earthly judges, the Lamb for our Passover. The trial of Jesus took place before two courts, the religious and the civil, the Jewish and the Roman, the Greater Sanhedrin and the Roman Procurator, Caiaphas and Pilate.

Strange, does it seem, that Jew and Gentile should both take a hand in this? For the Jew was the representative of religion at its purest, and Rome was the representative of justice at its highest. But it was meet that the religious and the civil, the spiritual and temporal, should both have a hand in this. Sin had entrenched itself in both realms, the spiritual and the civil, and the cross of Jesus has a message for both, and makes its impact on both. Jesus standing between Jew and Gentile, between Caiaphas and Pilate, was to unite both in the fellowship of a common salvation.

The Religious Authority

First, then, there was the religious authority. It was before Caiaphas, the judge with a spiritual jurisdiction, that Christ first appears; and it is in the religious sphere that the prime sentence of condemnation is passed. It is in the religious sphere that the crucifixion is planned. Sin-bearing, at its heart, is a spiritual reality, and the sin-bearer faces his trial and meets his condemnation there in the spiritual realm. And the charge against Jesus in the spiritual code is that of blasphemy, because he declared himself the Messiah. He is condemned on his own confession, which was contrary to Jewish practice and Jewish law; he is condemned on his own confession of being not only the Son of Man in his humiliation, but the Son of God in his coming glory.

So the Levitical Priesthood sat in judgement upon the Priest of another order, the one who was Priest after the order of Melchizedec, and they judged him on his own confession to be Son of Man and Son of God. They find him guilty of blasphemy, for which, in the religious code, the sentence was death. 'Messiah shall be cut off, but not,' said Daniel, 'for himself'. So the Levitical Priesthood examines the Lamb of God, finds no flaw in him, and passes on him the sentence of death.

The Temporal Authority

And then he goes to the temporal authority. Christ comes under the scrutiny of Pilate, and Pilate represents the civil and military authority of the powers that be. And so the spiritual power gives place to the civil, not to pass judgment, that has already been done, but to execute judgment. The Levitical Priesthood hands over the Melchizedec Priest to the temporal power to carry out the sentence of death.

There must be violence; the Roman sword must be in it. He must be 'wounded for our transgressions'. You see, when the priests decided that they could not carry out the sentence of death themselves, they must decide to refer the case to the Roman Governor, and so they had to decide what charge to proceed with before the Roman Court. A charge of blasphemy would be meaningless to Pilate; so they decided to alter the charge from religion to politics, from an offence against God to an offence against Caesar.

So Christ goes to Pilate as the Son of Man, and the charge is not religious, but civil and political. The spiritual always has its upheavals in the temporal, and the implications of the spiritual reach out always into the temporal. And so Pilate sets about to examine Jesus as a civil authority, and he examines him on the charge of being a rival to Caesar. It is a political case, but Christ brings the issue back where it belongs, into the spiritual. Before Pilate he acknowledges his spiritual Kingship: 'My kingdom is not of this world'.

'Art thou a king then?' asks Pilate.

'Yes', replied Jesus, 'to this end was I born, and for this cause came I into the world, that I should bear witness unto the truth.' He was born that he might wield the sceptre of truth.

Pilate is utterly lost in the spiritual sphere. He recognises nothing like truth in the temporal or civil sphere to which he belongs. It belongs really to the spiritual to which Pilate is an utter stranger, but Pilate pronounces judgement upon the man, 'I find no fault in him.' True, it was a negative judgment, it was of no value to Pilate himself. A negative relationship to Jesus leads to his crucifixion. But it is of value to us, he pronounces him fit to die!

Before we leave Pilate's court, there is an intervention that deeply moves us. It is that of Pilate's wife. We don't know who she was; tradition says her name was Procula; we don't know, but this noble woman puts in the last plea on the side of our Lord, and she dares to thrust herself between her fickle, unprincipled husband, and the foul deed to which he was to place his hand. Womanhood all over must look with admiration upon a noble woman who threw herself between her husband and his fate, and became the final intercessor for the Lord our Saviour.

The Verdict

But the spiritual works through the temporal, and Pilate sets about to execute the death sentence passed by the Sanhedrin. Only Rome, political mistress of the world, head of a world sovereignty, representative of world organisation, could carry out that sentence. As someone has put it, 'The brazen serpent is to be lifted up as high as the

Roman eagles could soar'. The impact of the death of Jesus must be felt by the world's organisation as a whole. So the jury brought in their verdict; they answered and said, 'He is guilty of death', and they all condemned him to be guilty of death. That's the verdict. And so the verdict in both courts was, 'Faultless, yet condemned to die'. Faultless, and so fit to die! He knew no sin, but he was made sin for us. He was chastised for our peace, condemned because of our rebellion, numbered with the transgressors. Made of a woman, made under the law, he is now condemned by the law as guilty of death.

The Prisoner

Now, that is the historical scene; but we are interested in the Prisoner rather than the process. Let us fix our eye for the moment upon the Prisoner.

There are contrasts here which are well nigh unintelligible until we know that he who knew no sin, was made sin for us, and that he was being chastised for our peace. There is, first, the amazing fact of his majesty and his submission. What he was in his own right, and what he was in his mediatorial function as the representative and surety of the transgressor, present us with a striking contrast. In all his relationships that day, it is the majesty of the Prisoner, his moral authority, that shines forth.

There was an outburst of this on the threshold of Gethsemane. In the Garden he was a broken Man, prostrate and crushed before the eye of his God, but when he faced his captors he said with infinite majesty, 'Whom seek ye?' And they replied, 'Jesus of Nazareth'. Then he announced himself - and you will see that the 'he' in your

Bibles is in italics, it is not in the original - he announced himself saying, not 'I am he', but 'I am'. And John adds, 'As soon as he had said 'I am', they went backward and fell to the ground'. On that occasion it was the 'I am' that spake, the Fellow of Jehovah, the One who even then stood by him, throned face to face in equal Deity; and at the announcement of the Divine Name, at the disclosure of the Divine Majesty, an outburst of power rushed through his Manhood, and they were broken men. No! They could not arrest Deity, man cannot touch God.

In like manner he moved through the proceedings with the dignity and authority of one who was judge rather than prisoner, who was disposing of events rather than himself the victim of circumstances. He never for one moment lost sight of the significance of the divine programme that was unfolding, a programme to which he had subscribed in eternal covenant, and which he was now to seal with his blood. 'Ye could do nothing', he said to Pilate, 'unless it were given to you from above.'

In that programme, human agents, men and devils, indeed had their appointed place. 'This is your hour and the power of darkness,' he said to his captors. He recognised that in the eternal programme of events, in the blueprint of redemption, his enemies on earth and in hell had an hour given to them in which to play the part permitted to them. An hour was reserved to them by heaven's permission, by the ruling of him to whom alone the hours belonged. For that brief hour, earth and heaven had their appropriate part to play. For that brief hour the earth became the centre of the moral universe, the stage on which events of eternal significance were to take place; and men and devils were actors in the events that were to resound through the whole universe of God. When man did his worst, he but fulfilled the eternal counsel of God. As Peter told the Jews after Pentecost, 'Him being delivered by the determinate counsel and foreknowledge of God, ye have taken, and by wicked hands have crucified and slain'. The deliberate counsel of man fulfilled the determinate counsel of God. Jesus' every action at this hour was in full accord with this consciousness, that the deliberate action of wicked men was but carrying out the determinate will and counsel of God.

But alongside this calm dignity, there was his unresisting submission. When his captors came to seek for him, and he saw the powers of the world, and of the underworld, coming into full array to do their worst, he could say, 'The prince of this world cometh and he hath nothing in me'. The prince of this world, the order of things in this evil world, had no ally in his breast, no foothold in his sinless nature. Yet he resists not, he is submissive to the divine will that is controlling the whole sequence of events. He is led as a lamb to the slaughter, unresisting, submissive, self-giving.

Another thing that strikes us about his conduct was his silence and his speech. It cannot be forgotten that the trial of Jesus took the form strictly of criminal proceedings. From that hour, when in the Garden Jesus had accepted the Cup, he was numbered with the transgressors openly and publicly. His legal state was that of a criminal and everything that fell to him he accepts as the portion of one who had to answer for the sins of many, who had to be chastised for our peace. It was a judicial change of state for him, even as justification is a judicial change of state for you and me.

He had to be delivered for our offensiveness. This will sufficiently explain his silence before his accusers. Through all the false witness borne against him, he maintained a majestic silence. He was acquiescing in the will of God; the sin he bore was inexcusable; as a sheep before her shearers, he was dumb.

As impressive as his silence is his speech. When the charge had broken down completely, the High Priest set to question the Prisoner, but before doing so, he administered the oath in Jewish fashion, 'I adjure thee by the Living God that thou tell us whether thou be the Christ, the Son of the Living God'. Brought thus into the presence of God, Christ could not maintain silence any longer, the great self-disclosure could no longer be delayed.

What a momentous hour, as the High Priest asks him, 'Who art thou? Tell us solemnly if thou be the Christ, the Son of the Living God'. And all the centuries bent down to catch the answer, for the hour for which the weary ages had been waiting had at last come, the self-disclosure of the Son of God, clothed in the vesture of sinful flesh. Fully conscious of its momentous meaning Christ solemnly takes the oath, using the familiar form, 'Thou sayest', it is as thou sayest.

The tension in the moral universe is suddenly relieved. He who is going to the altar has confessed himself to be the Christ, the Son of the Living God, the Priest and the sacrifice of the Household of Faith, and so this Melchizedec Priesthood is confirmed on earth by an oath. Then as Messiah, he disclosed the coming Glory, 'Hereafter, shall ye see the Son of Man sitting on the right hand of Power, and coming in the clouds of heaven.'

When Christ announces this, he is interpreting Old Testament prophecy, he is recognising himself as its full and final interpretation. In the Old Testament prophecy, Daniel tells of the breaking of the Messianic Kingdom, and till that comes, Jesus the Messiah is sitting on the right hand of Power, exercising a continuous process of government at the right hand of God. Thus his vindication as King lies behind the clouds; his sufferings and death pave the way to his enthronement, and his Coronation is utterly independent of the authority and the mandate of man. Yet he warns the Sanhedrin that day that the positions will be reversed, and one day they will appear before his throne - 'Ye shall see the Son of Man.'

Another contrast we find that we must note is the reality of the mockery meted out to him, the farce and the reality. That was part of the cruel suffering inflicted upon his sensitive nature - mockery. 'Reproach,' he said, 'hath broken my heart.' It seemed but rude, thoughtless, heartless buffoonery, but it wasn't merely that. It had a significance that went into the spiritual reality of things, even the mockery. For it is easy to see that he was being mocked in his threefold office as Prophet, Priest and King.

As Prophet when they spat in his face, blindfolded him, struck him, and cried 'Prophesy unto us, thou Christ, who is he that struck thee?' Sad, and full of sad significance, it is Israel that mocks, mocks her own Prophet, and with him, all her prophets that bore witness to him. In that mockery Israel turns her back on her glorious heritage of divine prophecy and revelation, and pours upon it her derision and her scorn.

As Priest he was mocked. Caiaphas had already unwittingly laid down the principle of substitutionary death when he counselled that 'it is expedient that one man should die for the people, and that the whole nation perish not'. Cynical words, but ominous words, with meaning far beyond the intention of the High Priest. Yet, despite this recognition, he is ridiculed and smitten in the presence of Annas because Truth was to him dearer than life. And from the cross he was taunted with the cry, the mocking cry, 'He saved others, himself he cannot save'.

As King he was mocked, both in the Hall of the High Priest, and by the soldiers of Herod who clothed him in purple and set him at nought. Christ before Herod captures the imagination. Herod Antipas was not a full-blooded Jew. He was an Idumean, and so a descendent, not of Jacob but of Esau. It is this fact that stirs the imagination. Long ago there was a struggle in the tent between Jacob and Esau over the birthright, over the right to be the progenitor of the Messiah, and Esau despised his birthright. Today, the seed of Jacob, the true Israel, stands before the seed of Esau; and the seed of Esau, in the person of Herod, once again mocks the Messiah. And Jesus is silent under the mockery.

Now, we must wait to ask, 'Was all this mockery the empty farce that it seemed?' Nothing that transpired in these eventful days could be deemed empty or meaningless. All had implications far beyond the reach of the naked eye to see. The Prophet of Israel whom his nation had covered with mockery, was, notwithstanding, God's supreme Prophet to his people, the last in the glorious line of prophets, and at that hour he was witnessing a good confession, bearing witness at that hour to the Truth, as Truth had never been witnessed to before. They had blindfolded him, but they could not blind him to the vision of his divine task. The eyes of his soul were wide open, and as the blows fell upon him, he knew he was chastised for our peace. They had blindfolded him, but witness he will deliver, and nothing can obscure his vision of the will of God for our salvation entrusted to his hands.

The Priest of Israel was made a pawn in the political fortunes of the nation; but Caiaphas, when he cynically counselled that Christ should die for the nation, spoke truer than he knew. It was what John calls a prophecy, forth-telling the ransom death of the Messiah. Singular was it, that the last Old Testament Priest should thus be pointing to the last Lamb and defining its function. When they flung the cruel taunt at him, 'He saved others, himself he cannot save', they laid bare the foundations of his Priesthood, self-sacrifice, and the cost of his blood.

The King is here. The one robed in purple, crowned with thorns, was indeed ascending his throne, and his crown was truly the thorns that were the emblems of our sin and our curse. What though the throne be a cross, from it he rules and governs his kingdom. With those pierced hands he lifted empires off their hinges, he stemmed the flowing tide of history, and he still, with those pierced hands, shapes and governs the ages.

All that mock drama enacted on the stage of time had an eternal significance, an eternal reality. He was chastised for our peace: peace to the mind, as truth comes from the Prophet's lips with illuming power; peace to the conscience, for the ransom is paid and the guilty set free; peace to the heart and life, as the King exercises his crown-rights from the cross, and raises his Royal Sceptre over the entire empire of our manhood and womanhood.

The blow that struck him reached him as he stood in our place, for he stood solitary over against God as the second Adam to receive the execution of the judgment pronounced upon the first Adam. When he was struck it was not a mere unit of the Race that was struck, not even a branch of the Race, it was its root, its head, its cornerstone; and the shock was felt at the very foundations of humanity.

But we cannot, we dare not, stay at a distance from this that is happening. He is chastised for our peace, he is passing under our condemnation, and no voice in heaven or earth can acquit him. He identified himself with our sin, its criminality passes over to him, and he bowed his head under the shame, the bitterness and the pain of our condemnation. Now, as we stand awed and bewildered at this that is happening to him, we hear the surge of glad tidings coming forth from his place of condemnation: 'There is therefore now no condemnation to them which are in Christ Jesus', and we enter into peace, 'the peace of God which passeth all understanding'.

CHAPTER 5

THE LAST OFFERING

His Body On the Tree

Let us think of the last offering, his body on the tree. We have already remarked that our Lord was throughout his entire life on earth a sin-bearer, and that he was right along fulfilling all his redemptive offices as Prophet, Priest and King, from the cradle to the grave. It is not legitimate for us to separate these functions and say, 'Now his Prophetic Office closes, and his Priesthood begins'. He was a King while he was offering his sacrifice, it was a Royal Priesthood; he was a Prophet revealing God while he was executing the Priestly Office; he was a Priest while he was fulfilling the Prophetic Office.

So the three offices of Christ, while they are distinct, are inseparable, and they do not refer to separate periods of his life and work; nor can we indeed accept him in one office and reject him in the other. There is a lot of foolish, loose talk about accepting Christ as Saviour but not accepting him as Lord and King. I think that is due to a merely intellectual view of faith. Spiritual faith, the faith of the entire soul, embraces Christ in his entirety. He is not divided. There may be distinctions and differences in our intellectual apprehension of the Christ we receive, but there can be no refusal of Christ as Priest or as Prophet or as King.

Christ is not divided, he is in his entirety the Saviour of the soul, and it is as the Saviour of the soul that faith receives him. We know that there is a development in our understanding and our apprehension, and our conscious possession of the blessedness we have received; for we have received, in a day of grace a whole Christ.

Nevertheless, we specially recognise him in each of these offices on special occasions. As a Prophet, for example, when delivering his Sermon on the Mount, and as a King when riding into Jerusalem; and we specially recognise his Priesthood as he approaches the altar and gives the Last Offering. He was always giving, but this was a final and a supreme offering when he gave himself unto death for us. For that reason we call this study the Last Offering, and it focuses our attention on the cross. Here we have unfolded a further aspect of what it meant to make atonement.

We have been pondering the theme of the cross in the experience of our Lord, but now we come to the heart of our subject, to the Last Offering. 'He was wounded for our transgressions' - there we have the gracious representation of the Second Adam. 'He was bruised for our iniquities' - there we got the mystery of imputation; 'he was chastised on account of our dispeace' - there we got the propitiation; and now, 'he endured sores for our healing' - there we get the expiation, the putting away completely of sin.

He endured *sores*. You remember we called it skin eruptions, as if a virulent poison had entered his bloodstream. There was not merely the sword that wounded him, nor the burden that crushed him, nor the rod that chastised him, there was also the Cup he drank. The Cup that passed before him in Gethsemane was now being drunk to its very

Not by Works of Righteousness

Dear Reader,

How do you hope to be saved?

Many are the answers which men give to the above question, but perhaps by far the commonest is as follows: 'I have never harmed anyone; I am doing the best I can. What more can God expect of me?' Or else: 'I try to live a good life and do my duty. I know there is no one perfect, but I'm no worse than others. Surely, God will accept me for what I am?'

Is this, more or less your answer? If it is, let me respectfully point out where you are going wrong, and I trust that you will take it kindly. If yours is the above answer, you are judging yourself by false standards and so you come to a false conclusion. This is something which we are all prone to do. We tend to compare ourselves with ourselves or else with others. Both these standards or tests are false. The true standard of judgement for life and conduct is the Word of God. To it, and not to ourselves or others, we must go if we are to be put right.

What, then, has the Word of God to say about this subject of salvation? It tells us that 'all have sinned and come short of the glory of God': that there is 'none righteous, no not one' (see Romans 3. 9-18). Even our good deeds are worthless as far as making us acceptable to God. He says that our 'righteousnesses are as filthy rags' in His sight.

Jesus once told a story about a Pharisee and a tax-collector both of whom went up to the temple to pray. The Pharisee in speaking to God, recounted all his good deeds. He thanked God that he was not like other men who were great sinners. He told God how he fasted twice in the week, and how he gave a tenth of his income to the church. You will notice that what he was dregs. What was the bitterness in that Cup? It was surely the curse of sin and all that it involved. It was the curse that made sin a disease in the spiritual life of man that needed his stripes to heal him.

Sin carries with it its own curse, and it is inherent in the very nature of sin. Its curse rests upon man's labours, for the ploughing of the wicked is sin; its curse rests upon his environment, for the ground is cursed because of his sin. It therefore sends its disease everywhere, bringing a physical, moral and spiritual blight in its wake. And it is this curse we now see put away, exhausted, expiated, by the sufferings on the tree, when he 'his own self, bore our sins consciously in his body on the tree'.

Sin is there a curse, and that surely brings us to the very heart of the work of atonement, to the Curse-bearer, and the Curse-absorber. As we view the cross, there are five aspects that I would like to present to you. First of all, the place of the Curse, outside the Gate; second, the instrument of the Curse, the cross; third, the expression of the Curse, darkness; fourth, the essence of the Curse, desertion; and fifth, the exhaustion of the Curse, death.

The Place of the Curse

First of all, then, the place of the Curse. It is highly significant that when the sentence of death was passed upon Jesus within the city of Jerusalem, he was led outside the city to die. It would seem as if the Jews, at the last, were forsaking the exclusiveness of the centuries, and putting their most precious gift outside the Gate within the reach of all. Or, was it that they were giving expression to the terrible fact that they had no place for him in death, as they

85

had no place for him in his life, that they were dissociating themselves from the spiritual significance and the healing virtue of his death? Perhaps, but I think it is better to recognise God in it, and the operation of those eternal principles that lie behind and beneath the work of atonement. The finger of God is in it. This was the place of the Curse, where the carcasses, the offal of the beasts given in sacrifice were burned. They had to be taken outside the camp inasmuch as they were symbolically involved in the curse of the sin-bearing. And he was that Curse-bearing Lamb.

There is one illustration of this from the Old Testament ritual that I would like to say a word about to you. It is the perfect illustration because it is God's. You know that the sacrifices of the Old Testament give us the inside story of Calvary. They are like X-ray plates of the cross. They, of course, were shadows, but so are X-ray plates, shadows cast upon delicately prepared plates; but when you look at them in the light you will see the inside story of your pain, and of your weakness, and of your illness. So the sacrifices of the Old Testament were, in reality, shadows. But they were penetrating shadows, X-ray plates of the mystery of Calvary, and when you look at them in the light of the gospel, you will read the inside story of his suffering and of your redemption.

One of these, I think, was significant because it was a compound sacrifice - it took two animals to make up the sacrifice. Two kids of the goat were taken, each designed for a specific end. The first kid was taken by the Priest and brought at once to the altar of God, and there its blood was shed, and its life was forfeit. That kid dealt with sin God-wards, in all its guilt, and the wages of sin were meted out - death.

But the other kid was treated differently. The one

offering it, or the High Priest in his name, placed his hands on the head of the kid, and so, in a figure, transferred sin from himself to the sin-bearer. And that animal, being a sin-bearer, became accursed. Its blood was not shed. Death, you know, would not extinguish the 'worm that dieth not', and 'the fire that is not quenched'. The Curse-bearer must be sent away, and he was carried by the hands of a fit man into the wilderness, and there, in the far reaches of the desert, untracked by human foot, the curse-bearing kid is let loose, left alive; but he is never seen again, and he never returns to the flocks of Israel. The Curse of sin is borne away to a land of forgetfulness, a land from which there can be no return.

Need I say that, as both constituted the one sacrifice, so both find their fulfilment in the one sacrifice of Calvary, and in the experience of our Lord Jesus Christ? Being a sin-bearer he must deal with God, and God requires that blood should be shed. The wages of sin is death, and the sin-bearing Lamb must die. But he also bears the Curse of sin in his own deepest experience, and that Curse brings him into a land of far distances where he separates himself from mankind, and enters into a wilderness that is devastated and blighted by the Curse of sin, by the indignation of God, and by the wrath of the Eternal. That wilderness, untracked by the foot of man, was his dwelling place for those dark hours he spent on the tree. Both meet in Jesus, death and the life that cannot die, for he truly was the one who could die, and yet go living through all the experience of death, both the Lamb slain, and a Curse-bearing one that could not die. And so Christ, as the scapegoat of the New Covenant, was taken outside the habitations of the living, into the desolation of the place called Calvary, and there he entered into the experiences of what curse-bearing must mean. That is the place appropriate to the curse.

The Instrument of the Curse

The second thing we were to consider was the instrument of the Curse. The Curse was being exhibited to the world, and ministered to himself by the instrumentality of the cross. Without doubt, Christ himself interpreted the cross in that light; and God viewed the cross in that light; and the masses of the Jewish people viewed it in that light too.

It is strange indeed that it should be death by crucifixion that was meted out to him - that was not the Jewish form of capital punishment, but the Roman. And the balance of power between the Jews and the Romans was such that the Jews could pass sentence, and the Romans reserve to themselves the right to review it, and to execute it. Hence the Priest could say, 'We have a law, and by our law he must die'. And Pilate in effect could say: 'If he is to die, he shall die in our way, not in yours!' Hence, in the providence of God, it came about that he was not stoned to death, for 'not a bone of him should be broken'. But he was crucified that men might 'look upon him whom they had pierced'.

The deepest significance of the cross was that it was symbolic of the Curse of sin, and that through it, the bitterness, the anguish, the desolation of that Curse should be ministered to the heart and soul of our Lord. Early in his ministry he realised the implications of this when he compared himself to the impaled serpent that Moses uplifted in the wilderness. Daily it made him a Man of Sorrows and acquainted with grief. Again and again its dark shadow fell across the road he trod, but its final realisation entered his deepest consciousness only on the tree, where he became accursed for us, an object of disdain and ridicule and mockery, cast out by earth and rejected by heaven - the Curse-Bearer! That is the instrument of the Curse - the cross.

The Expression of the Curse

Third, the expression of the Curse. The Curse experienced in the spiritual consciousness of Christ, had, like most other spiritual realities on this occasion, an outward expression. For example, it was no accident that he should, in his dying hour, be given a central place among thieves, as if he were the greatest malefactor of them all. It is strange, of course. It gives us a jolt to reflect that he, who began his life in the cradle among gold and frankincense and myrrh, surrounded by the adoration and the worship of wise and saintly men, should now be ending it in the company of thieves, among the oaths and curses of tortured men. What a reversal of fortune!

But there is a needs be - he was outwardly and publicly 'numbered with the transgressors'. Christ is going to the altar as a sacrifice for the world's sin, and in sin-bearing he is accursed. And our High Priest on his way to the altar has, as his companions, not two Levites, but two malefactors. The Levitical Priesthood stands at a distance, its function is over, it can only point to the supreme sacrifice. He alone can accomplish this that he is undertaking, and in this transaction he is Priest, and Altar and Sacrifice.

But the most impressive expression of the Curse was this that happened when he was on the tree: 'And there was darkness over all the earth until the ninth hour'. There were three hours of darkness, from twelve noon till three o'clock.

But it was not measured by time; it was an infinite transaction that was taking place, it was the Infinite Person of the Son of God that was engaged. It was very significant that when the extreme sacrifice was about to be offered, God stretched out his hand, and drew a curtain over the face of the sun. It was obviously the direct intervention of God, not as an expression of sorrow, not a garment of mourning cast over the world; rather does it express the imposing of judgment upon the lonely, outcast Sufferer. That darkness was to him the true expression of the Curse.

Christ, in that transaction, was stepping over the borderline in his soul's experience. He was going outside the gates of life and light, he was being thrust into night; and it was alone with God in the dark that that final transaction took place. His dealings with men are finished, now he is dealing with God alone, with God for men. Read the Book of Revelation to see there outpoured the seven vials of the last judgment of God. The last judgment has projected itself into the experience of Jesus, he is even now under the judgment of God, and the seven vials of wrath are being emptied into his inmost soul. Who of mankind can tell what happened in these three hours of outer night? There is a wonderful phrase in the liturgy of the Greek Church which says, 'By thine unknown suffering, good Lord deliver us.' Unknown and unknowable!

Our minds travel back to the first creation when darkness covered the earth, and the Divine fiat went out, 'Let there be light!' Once again a darkness covers the earth as the Son of God is laying down the foundations of a second Creation, and preparing the way for the second fiat, as the light of the knowledge of the Glory of God streams into darkened hearts from the face of a crucified Saviour.

To us, what does all this mean? Luke, again, with his customary sensitiveness, in one bold stroke unites two great phenomena of that hour: 'and the sun was darkened, and the veil of the Temple was rent in the midst'. What a wondrous combination: Darkness for him, and a rent veil for you and me! Darkness for him, light for us; exclusion for him, access for the sinner.

The Essence of the Curse

Fourthly, the essence of the Curse. The darkness was only a pall, an outward covering, both expressing and concealing what was happening there. As we said, we can never fully know what happened. But this we know, that from the darkness there came a heart-rending cry of a Saviour in anguish, 'My God, my God, why hast thou forsaken me?' There was a divine desertion in it, and that was the very quintessence of the Curse. But could it really happen? God could not forsake God, could he? But God had forsaken the sin-bearer, and it was real. It was not a sense of something that did not happen, it was not merely subjective.

The Christian may feel forsaken, but it is purely subjective. He may have a sense of being forsaken when it is only a withdrawal of the divine presence and peace. But here the situation was entirely different. The forsakenness of Christ was a reality, not merely subjective; not merely that he felt forsaken, he *was* forsaken. God was active in that forsakenness, God was withdrawing himself. Men, righteous men on earth, under the chastisement of God may feel forsaken, but they can anchor their hope on the promise, 'I will never leave thee, nor forsake thee'. But this Man had no such anchorage. Heaven had closed its doors against him. No angel comes out now to give him comfort, no message from Home to cheer him in his desolation and loneliness, but rather a silence that was more dreadful than speech. And why? Christ brings his plea to God, he presents his 'Why?' He wanted to have the eternal principles of holy rectitude and justice laid bare, 'Why hast thou forsaken me?' Christ was forsaken because of his relationship to sin, to a broken law, to judgment, and to the Curse. And the abandonment was complete.

Of course, he was not separated from God, ' God was in Christ', at that hour, 'reconciling the world to himself.' But he has laid down a basis on which others could never be forsaken, a basis on which the promise could stand secure, 'I will never leave thee, nor forsake thee'. That was the essence of the Curse: a desertion, an abandonment, a withdrawal of the fellowship and the face of God, even when God was in Christ transacting this for us men and for our salvation.

The Exhaustion of the Curse

Then lastly, its exhaustion: death. The Curse had to be exhausted, but only by expiation. He must die death outright, and it was no ordinary death; not the mere separation of soul and body. All that death meant was experienced before soul and body were separated. It is said that he 'tasted death for every man'; every man's death, the poison of all death, was concentrated in his Cup. In that outer darkness the vapours of death had penetrated his very being, but he would hold nothing back, he must go the whole road; and in his body, in his exquisitely tender self-consciousness, he endured and accepted it all. Death was softened for others, even for the malefactors at his side, but not for him. They offered him a sedative, wine mingled with myrrh, a partial anaesthetic, the only soporific of that day, wine with myrrh; but he took it not. His consciousness must not be blunted; like the scapegoat he must go alive through death.

But his physical nature was apparently weakening, and yet he cannot falter till the Last Offering is given. He must die in full possession of all his faculties and all his exquisite sensitiveness to pain. For it was a vicarious suffering, the one for the many. He cried 'I thirst' - the outer expression of an inner anguish. And they gave him sour wine, the Roman soldier's common drink. When exhausted and wearied on the march, the soldier's drink was sour wine. He took it. It revived him for the last stupendous effort. He rallied all his physical and spiritual forces, and he laid himself upon the altar as the Last Offering. And then, with a loud voice, he cried, 'It is finished'.

Life did not ebb away, it was given. In full possession of all he ever had, he laid that all upon the altar, a whole burnt-offering unto God. He maintained the tension to the close, nor did it slacken till he gave that last triumphant cry. In full possession of his strength and fortitude he entered upon the last step of his humiliation, the last mile of a dark and desolate road, till the Curse was exhausted, till the Cup was drained dry. In a last act of unshaken trust, he committed his spirit into the arms of his God; arms that were underneath him all the time, for, 'God was in Christ'. So he made an end of sin, and brought in an everlasting righteousness.

There is one note that we must catch before we leave this scene. Our Lord was crucified in weakness, dying, he was forsaken and outcast. He cried unto God, and he seemed not to be answered. He knocked at his Father's door, and there was no response. Then, a dying malefactor appealed to his power to save, and immediately, without hesitation, he gave him the promise, 'Today shalt thou be with me in Paradise.' He was excluded himself for a brief season when 'he bore the sins of many'; but he had a right to take a guest home with him without asking leave of any. He had the key to the Father's door in his pierced hand. He could open and no man shut, he could shut and no man open; and the guest he took home with him to his Father's table that day was the first trophy of Calvary after the sacrifice had been finished. Crucified in weakness, he was mighty to save.

These scenes around the cross have a penetrating significance. Often I feel there is not a single figure that surrounds the cross but has its representative in the world today, as it has had throughout all the ages. Personally, I think that of all who were in the vicinity of the cross that day, I would rather be in the shoes of Barabbas. Barabbas had a wonderful angle on the cross; he could point to the middle cross and say, 'There would I have been, if he hadn't been put in my place.'

What shall we say, then, to these things? Let me quote you one passage from Hebrews 13:12, 'Wherefore Jesus also, that he might sanctify the people with his own blood, suffered outside the gate'; the fact that provides a broad basis of our Christian religion, and then there is the divine interpretation of the fact: 'that he might sanctify the people with his own blood'.

And what is the appropriate response that God expects from you and me? 'Let us therefore go unto him outside the Camp, bearing his reproach.' That is the whole of the Christian life, going and bearing, going and bearing, going *outside* the Camp. A crucified Saviour has never been taken in! They have tried to put garlands on his cross, they have tried to perfume the rude and accursed tree. But no, in its naked ugliness, an unmasking of human guilt and shame, the cross is still outside. The condemnation of the sinner is still outside the gate.

And you and I have gone there. The day we believed in Jesus as the Saviour of our souls, he took us outside the Camp. There was a time when you thought your salvation could be found inside, but you proved it false. When you looked for salvation without, you felt a drawing power that broke your link with the Camp, and bound you to him who died upon the tree, and you identified yourself with the sin he bore, and you reached to him in adoration, and gratitude, and faith, saying, 'He loved me, and gave himself for me.' You found yourself, even you, at the heart and centre of his love and his sacrifice.

And then, as you go to worship him, you daily reach him outside. Is there no worship of Christ inside the Camp? Oh yes! You remember how they worshipped him there. They took off him his own seamless robe. It had stains of blood, for he had been scourged. They put on him a shabby robe of purple; they put a crown of thorns upon his head, and a sickly reed in his hand; then they bowed the knee saying 'Hail', and 'they worshipped him'.

That is the worship that is given to your Lord inside the Camp to this day. They rob him of his bloodstained robe, and they put on him the shabby robe of human sentimentality and human goodness. They put their own crown upon his brow, and their own reed in his hand. But that is not the Christ who saved your soul. He is outside the Camp, you worship him there.

Yes, and when you serve him, you go there. 'Oh', but you say, 'I don't believe that. I think that service, service to Christ, means really staying inside and making the best of the situation there, and bearing a brave witness whenever I can. I believe in meeting men on their own ground, and I believe in joining with them as far as I can go. And I believe in making myself agreeable and participating in their affairs as far as I can.'

Well, you know, I'm in a dilemma. In theory I can't find a flaw in that, but in practice it just never works. It's been a complete failure since Lot tried it in Sodom! And what then am I to do? If you want to serve your Redeemer, go unto him outside the Camp; get his commission for your service, get the ordination of his pierced hands, and come back to the Camp bearing the light of his authority in your face, and say, 'Thus saith the Lord.' And men will take knowledge of you that you have been with Jesus.

That is the endowment and the enduement for effective service, the power that comes from without. And you are telling men of the Christ you met there outside the Gate!

Going and bearing, 'bearing his reproach'. What is the reproach of Christ? I cannot tell. It is not the same to any two people. What might be a reproach to me wouldn't be a reproach to you at all. But I think this is it: The reproach is that you dare to go outside the Camp, that you dare to be different, that you dare to break with the life of the Camp. That's the reproach. Are you afraid of being different? Pause a minute. If he endured the cross in all its bitterness, in all its pain, in all its curse, isn't it a little matter that you should share with him the reproach. Nay, is it not an honour an angel might covet, to be asked to share his reproach?

Let us, therefore, go unto him.